D0900047

hustle

Bonnie Ullman

Sal Kibler

for Mark + Jack,
Everything you need
to know about marketing
to women is in here!
Read carefully.

Marketing to Women in the
Post-Recession World

hustle

BONNIE ULMAN

SAL KIBLER

Paramount Market Publishing, Inc.

Paramount Market Publishing, Inc.

950 Danby Road, Suite 136

Ithaca, NY 14850

www.paramountbooks.com

Phone: 607-275-8100; 888-787-8100

Fax: 607-275-8101

Publisher: James Madden

Editorial Director: Doris Walsh

Copyright © 2013 Bonnie Ulman & Sal Kibler

Printed in USA

All rights reserved. No part of this book may be reproduced, stored in a retrieval system, or transmitted in any form or by any means, electronic, mechanical, photocopying, recording, or otherwise, without the prior written permission of the publisher. Further information may be obtained from Paramount Market Publishing, Inc., 950 Danby Road, Suite 136, Ithaca, NY 14850.

This publication is designed to provide accurate and authoritative information in regard to the subject matter covered. It is sold with the understanding that the publisher is not engaged in rendering legal, accounting, or other professional services. If legal advice or other expert assistance is required, the services of a competent professional should be sought.

All trademarks are the property of their respective companies.

Cataloging in Publication Data available

ISBN-10: 0-9851795-2-X | ISBN-13: 978-0-9851795-2-6

To my late grandmothers Norma Worthy and Pauline Hammond—"steel magnolias" who embodied grace, courage, strength and love and never used the Great Depression as an excuse to give up.

BONNIE ULMAN

In memory of my mother Lila Salisbury Henley and my mother-in-law Caroline Dykes Kibler, innocent girls of the Depression who became strong, inspirational women of the modern world. You continue to inspire me every day.

SAL KIBLER

Contents

Preface   ix

1   Farewell   1

2   Jolt   11

3   Hustle   21

4   Escape Hatches   31

5   Trading Down   40

6   Sway   51

7   Screens   61

8   Sages   69

9   Seers   78

10   2020 in 20/20   89

Acknowledgments   93

Endnotes   97

Index   103

About the Authors   107

Preface

My mother is one of those individuals who can manufacture anything out of the items she has on hand. She was Green way before Green was in vogue. The poster child for repurposing, she used salvaged windows when we renovated the basement of our home and ground down Coca-Cola bottles for the kids to use as drinking glasses. As a child I marveled at the jars of orphaned buttons, half-yard fabric remnants, and odds and ends that found their way into our house. Over time, marvel morphed into mockery and as a teen I poked fun at my mom's pack rat sensibilities.

Not long ago, mom called and asked for help cleaning out her garage. "It is time to sort things out," she said. Not an easy task for someone who is an über-gatherer by nature. She began by handing me a box of Mason jars she'd been keeping to can figs from a tree out back. Then on to the next box that held artwork from my preschool days and yearbooks from high school. Sorting led to reminiscing and for the first time I began to see how the impact of being a woman who grew up in the shadow of the Great Depression had taken hold and profoundly informed who she is 70-plus years later.

In my profession as a consultant advising companies on marketing to women and mothers, I have unique opportunities to talk with women on a continual basis in casual settings and through formal research situations. We discuss their attitudes and behaviors, brand preferences and dislikes, and the driving forces shaping the decisions they make. As our most recent economic downturn—the Great Recession—kicked in to high gear, my colleagues and I began hearing nuanced changes in the way women were talking about life—in ways not all that different from women describing the Great Depression. As conversations progressed, we were compelled to follow the trail further by conducting original research that led us to the conclusion that the Great Recession has created significant and lasting impacts on women and imprinted their attitudes and beliefs; how they buy, what they buy, and their relationship with brands. What began as idle curiosity morphed in to active surveillance and then took flight as a full-scale research exploration.

Early in the project, I called Sal Kibler, a long-time friend and colleague and a gifted thinker whose insights and perceptions are always keen and prescient. In talking through what was a germ of an idea, Sal began recounting stories of her own mom and joined in the project as contributing author.

This book—Hustle—is the result of qualitative and quantitative research conducted with thousands of women coast-to-coast who represent a wide swath of socio-economic groups, ages and life stages, and myriad cultural backgrounds. Some are just entering the workforce, while others are exiting. Many have children and spouses, while an equal number are childless or parenting without a partner. These women, who shared their innermost fears and aspirations, reflect backgrounds that are a true kaleidoscope of society's cultural, religious, and socioeconomic planes.

Hustle is not a recap of the economics of the Great Recession, but an illustration for marketers of the long-lasting emotional, physical, and psychological effects of one of our country's worst economic downturns. In the end, our hope is to provide clarity around how to earn a fair share-of-wallet.

As professionals who have each worked in the marketing and communications fields for more than a quarter of a century, Sal and I have experienced the natural ups and downs of the market, survived more than a few sleepless nights, and come out the other side with more than a handful of witty stories. But this economic downturn has been different. The duration and depth ambushed women and as a result knocked loose the structure we all counted on to achieve productive, enjoyable lives. So what changes within a woman who is nearly always responsible for making the purchases in her home and is often the breadwinner in the household funding the purchases? Almost everything. She has a new emotional default that is geared to the negative. Her self-confidence is waning. Her belief in institutions and people—even those closest to her—is vapor. She hears, sees, and processes messages differently and requires a new level of commitment from those companies, products, services, brands, and even people she is willing to engage.

In our "real" jobs as consultants, we have begun building client marketing and communications strategies on the insights we've teased from the research. We share what we've learned in the following pages. *Hustle* was written as a resource for marketers, advertisers, communications and public relations professionals, digital and social media experts, business owners and entrepreneurs, corporate sales departments, academia, and brand marketing teams within companies and corporations, be they multinationals or tomorrow's start-up home runs. It is our sincere hope that you find it a helpful tool.

To the women who bared their unvarnished emotions and thoughts: without you, this book would be nothing more than an idea with no backbone. The authors profoundly thank you. And to the woman who inspired this research excavation, you are profoundly loved.

—Bonnie Ulman

March 2013

chapter 1

Farewell

A squirrel can change direction at lightning-swift speed, scampering across a lawn then up a tree in no time flat, which is what makes the word "squirrel" so ideal when describing the distraction of the American consumer during the 36 months leading up the Great Recession. A dray of squirrels, spun through a swollen current of commercial messages and a continual feed of legitimate news and infotainment. Combined with society's focus on acquisition, a strong financial marketplace, and an expanding job market, it's not difficult to understand why women didn't seem to notice the severity of the crack that was forming in the nation's economic house and in their own homes.

Penny Goodman is a 36-year-old who is on an executive leadership fast track at her company while balancing the needs of her husband and 10-year-old daughter. "Back in 2006, life was full. I was thrilled to have been chosen for a leadership program in my company and my family was flourishing at home. I didn't really have much time to think about or plan for anything else. Chasing the dream can be a full-time preoccupation," she said.

> "Back in 2006, life was full . . . I didn't really have much time to think about or plan for anything else. **Chasing the dream can be a full-time preoccupation.**"
>
> *Penny Goodman*

Penny's story is similar to those belonging to the hundreds of women we interviewed and the 1,000 women polled as part of an online research panel. Conducted in partnership with LiveWire Research, we found that 70 percent of women surveyed say they were surprised by the severity and duration of the Great Recession, too busy and distracted to recognize the signs signaling the severity of the impending economic meltdown. Young women between the ages of 24 and 29, who are just beginning careers or working to establish a lifestyle seemed to be even more impacted, with 79 percent reporting they were caught off guard by the significance of the downturn. From a cultural standpoint, Asian women (79 percent) seemed to be more surprised than Caucasians, African-Americans, and Hispanics about the severity and duration of the Recession, while Hispanic women were the least surprised (66 percent).

SURPRISED?

Percent of women who say they were surprised by the **severity** and **duration** of the Great Recession

all women surveyed:
70 percent

Asian women and women aged 24-29:
79 percent

Hispanic women:
66 percent

It wasn't until December 2008 that economists declared that the U.S. recession had actually begun some twelve months before, in December 2007.[1] By then the women we interviewed said they already felt there was a dynamic financial movement at play, especially the early impact on the economy they cared most about—their household economy. If they didn't feel it in their paychecks yet, they knew someone who had. The mean net worth of family incomes from 2007 through 2010 diminished by more than a third.[2] In the April 2011 *Monthly Labor Review*, economists Christopher J. Goodman and Steven Mance wrote, "The recent downturn is unique in that it is the first on record to have erased all of the jobs gained in the previous economic expansion."[3] Many of the women we spoke with reflected on their expectation of a *market correction*, not a *market catastrophe*.

platinum: the "wealth effect" of the housing boom

Willa John, a 50-year-old real estate broker in Southern California, summed up the years leading up to the Great Recession as *platinum.* "Those years, 2005 and 2006, were really spectacular. My clients viewed the economy as limitless—and honestly, I shared the sentiment. Everyone in the industry was working hard, not because we were scrambling to get a listing, but scrambling to keep up with the full pipeline of buyers and sellers," she shared. "Homes were selling for top dollar and many of us were pulling down big commissions. There really wasn't any time to think about where the country was headed. Our heads were down and we were hustling for the deal. My life then was really good. I can tell you that I really miss those days."

In 2006, housing growth was still a driver in the economy as more and more people achieved the American dream. "The rapid growth in housing construction led to job growth in construction as well as in complementary industries," Goodman and Mance said. And the housing boom, they continued, "had a 'wealth effect' on the economy. Real estate assets had grown by more than a third between 2001 and 2005." Homeowners, feeling flush with equity and enjoying lower interest rates, began extracting that wealth and plowing it into financing other things, including automobiles and consumer goods.

Consumer trend spotter Cynthia R. Cohen described her take on the disposition of the American consumer in 2006 in an article for ChiefMarketer.com.[4] Referring to "wacky, wily consumers," Cynthia made the point that pre-Great Recession consumers were enjoying a savory life and engineering lifestyles heavily predicated on celebrating the best that life had to offer: Ourselves. A half-dozen years ago, Cynthia forecasted a set of behaviors that promoted consumers' need to embrace our own uniqueness, tastes, and drive to collect information, experiences, and all that was cool, from "dressing for excess" and "bringing on the bling" to cherishing our bodies and palettes through "super foods" and "anything artisanal." We carved out opportunities to express our uniqueness and thirst for information and innovation with bedazzled witticisms emblazoned across our chests and top-dollar adventure travel packages reflecting our personal niche interests.

the emotional euphoria of the time: affluence

Based on the results of the annual Yesawich, Pepperdine, Brown & Robinson/Yankelovich Leisure Travel Monitor survey, *Travel Weekly* magazine identified a key trend for 2006—the mainstreaming of affluence, writing, "These days, virtually anybody can afford a taste of luxury, an ocean view, a private balcony, an afternoon at the spa. As a result, ordinary consumers are becoming more discerning."[5]

Our passion for over-the-top and exotic styles and products was also reflected in beauty and fashion. The higher-priced classics brought us some twists—Black Satin nail polish from Chanel and classic black wing tips embellished with skull and crossbones—that gave us ways to show we had the money but not in a stodgy way. The "all about me" mood was underscored in the selection of "YOU" as *Time* magazine's 2006 "Person of the Year," reflecting the power that individuals have in creating the content that is regularly shared with the world.

Even consumers who wouldn't be characterized as wealthy by economists' standards were acting on the emotional euphoria of the time. In his book, *Trading Up: The New American Luxury* (Portfolio, 2003), co-authored with Neil Fiske, Michael J. Silverstein described consumers' willingness to pay a significant premium for goods and services, especially those that were emotionally important to them and that delivered the perceived values of quality, performance, and engagement. He wrote:

> "America's middle-market consumers are trading up. They are willing, even eager, to pay a premium price for remarkable kinds of goods that we call New Luxury—products and services that possess higher levels of quality, taste, and aspiration than other goods in the category but are not so expensive as to be out of reach."[6]

An endless stream of tales documented the scene at retailer doors across America, where the mash of consumers who lined up for days preceding the launch of the coveted Sony PlayStation3 jockeyed for prime position, all for the privilege of being among the first to own the gaming console. Urban legend holds that one man—certain there wouldn't be enough hardware to go around—did the only logical thing he could think of: he treated people ahead of him in line to coffee laced with laxatives. He got his PlayStation3.

The heady times had Tween girls and their helicopter moms stalking the Hannah Montana cultural experience. In technology, we became further empowered and entertained through the iPhone and Halo, while *The Devil Wears Prada* gave us an insider's view of the power and influence of the fashion world and its players.

There were few slow news days in 2005 and 2006. A steady stream of worthy headline events from across America and around the world filled the news cycle, overshadowing the early forecasts of shaky economic times ahead. A dozen workers sadly lost their lives in the Sago Mine disaster in January leading to questions about safety and inspections. The execution of Saddam Hussein was made available for viewing moments after the act via YouTube, leading to questions about judgment and humanity. We watched in disbelief as

New Orleans stayed flooded for weeks and the establishment seemed impotent in their response. The milestone of the 3,000th American casualty in Iraq was announced in December of 2006 with little fanfare. Republican Congressman Mark Foley brought a new kind of sex scandal to Washington and in a blow to all who learned the mnemonic "My Very Energetic Mother Just Served Us Nine Pizzas" as a way to recall planetary order, Pluto lost its status as a grown up planet, downgraded to dwarf.

> It should have been apparent, but we didn't really **connect the dots.**

A foreshadowing of the deterioration or distraction by some of our most trusted institutions should have been apparent, but we didn't really connect the dots to the impending economy downturn. Current history affirmed for us that economic downturns come and go with some regularity and we always seem to survive and even, ultimately, thrive.

Andrea Boutelle is an accomplished woman with a heart as big as her home state of Texas. She doesn't recall the date the Great Recession was declared, but she has perfect clarity about the day it walked through her front door. "My husband had been with his company, a pharmaceutical company, for a long time. He had worked his way up through the ranks and was good at his job. Then one day, he was downsized. That was one of those moments when time stands still, a vivid memory," she says.

> "Looking back, the signs had been there, but you're **never really prepared."**
> *Andrea Boutelle*

"Looking back, the signs had been there, but you're never really prepared. This has all had a lasting effect on me, my husband, and our children. We question everything."

The push to fulfill and the mental and emotional filters women used to process news contributed to an inability or failure for many to interpret the severity of the advance warnings about an impending economic downturn. In mid-2006, cracks in the veneer of corporate America began to deepen, brought into sharp focus when the greed of Enron executives was exposed. On May 25, 2006, former Enron executives Kenneth Lay and Jeffrey Skilling were found guilty of fraud and conspiracy, acts that led to the loss of 20,000 jobs and retirement and life savings of many unsuspecting Enronites. The housing bubble burst. Homeowners began defaulting on subprime mortgages, kicking off a string of mortgage company failures. Banks that had supported mortgage-backed securities were left with worthless investments. In December 2007, consumers pulled back with sharply decreased personal consumption that showed economic anxiety across the socio-economic spectrum. By September 2008, Lehman Brothers investment banking collapsed, triggering the fall of a long series of financial services and related industry sector giants. While the Recession was officially declared over in June of 2009,[7] the hemorrhaging continued in the most personal way for women through loss of jobs for themselves, their families, their neighbors.

The facts and figures that economists used to forecast the Great Recession are largely lost on the women who shared their stories with us. For them, the Great Recession was a bullet train—rapid, powerful and stealthy. When the pieces began to crumble, women just weren't prepared. They initially answered the uncertainty with one of two responses: hit the bunker or bury my head in the sand.

Depressions: the great and the near great

Experts and media compare the present-day Recession with the Great Depression of the 1920s and 1930s. The events leading up to both are similar and the collateral damage on the housing market and confidence in financial institutions are alike. When you examine the fall-out of the two economic downturns, what we found profoundly interesting wasn't in the DNA of the marketplace but buried in the psyche of the women whose lives were altered.

Benjamin Schwarz, literary editor and national editor for *The Atlantic*, wrote a bellwether article for the magazine, entitled "Life In (and After) our Great Recession." His piece referenced a number of experts and publications that describe the emotional toll of the Great Depression, which he uses to draw parallels with the current Great Recession. Schwarz refers to one of the defining books about the impact of the Great Depression, *Middletown in Transition* by Robert S. and Helen Merrell Lynd (Harcourt, Brace & Company, 1982), which chronicles an Indiana town muddling through the Great Depression, to provide context for his conclusions:

"... but all of these accounts agree on one workaday detail of middle-class life: the effort to maintain the highest-possible standard of material living in an age of reduced circumstances meant that the physical burden of the new normal fell overwhelmingly on women. The hours of what were then called servants were cut, or those workers were fired altogether (just as is now happening with the hours and jobs of housekeepers, nannies, and—at least here in Southern California—gardeners), but the tasks they performed remained to be done. And 'domestic' work that had previously been performed outside the home shifted to the household. Home-baked bread replaced store-bought; home preserving became de rigueur. Clothes and household items were mended rather than replaced."

Today, the twice-weekly takeout dinners from Boston Market or the Whole Foods deli counter, along with the regular expeditions to

California Pizza Kitchen or Outback Steakhouse, have been reduced, and children and adults are more frequently brown-bagging their lunches—which means that more meals are prepared at home. Eighty years ago, it was wives and mothers who overwhelmingly took up the slack. Surprise, surprise: little has changed today.[8]

a new kind of American household

As with the Great Depression, the Great Recession has spurred a new kind of American household that cannot be defined in the classic sense for marketers. In some ways it mirrors that of the Great Depression. There is a stagnation of new household formation and a declining birthrate.[9] The retro household may be in a smaller footprint but with a larger population. It is not expanding out to create new households, but holding its own with adult children boomeranging back in and other relatives knocking at the front door. The number of 26-year-olds living with their parents has jumped almost 46 percent since 2007.[10] More than 60 percent of adults aged 25 to 34 know friends of family members who have moved back in with a parent or set of parents, creating a multi-generational household.[11] If you are a marketer who is basing your strategy on driving spending, these sharply turned trends are working against you.

# of 26-year-olds living with their parents:

▲ 46% since 2007

However, the post-Recession household offers new opportunities for brands to bring renewed pleasure and purpose into these rede-fined households and to engender brand appreciation. As families relearn how to get along without a private bathroom or car for each individual, marketers can help find ways to give each individual some power within their own space, technology, closet, or backpack.

the opportunities in "frugality fatigue"

The fatigue of frugality is real. Women are looking for a reprieve with new and innovative products and tips that will help them create real experiences with and for their families that are within economic reach. Do not underestimate the far-reaching impact of stress, fatigue, and sometimes resentment, that today's woman carries. For many, the Great Recession is the Great Repression, convincing many women that they have lost a measure of control over their lives. Women are natural pilots and find satisfaction in captaining their family and household accounts. If your game plan is to tell her what to buy based on features and price, then you need to rethink your strategy. Today's consumer wants you to give her options for redesigning her life. Ways that are leaner and meaner. Ways that make her feel smarter than ever before.

> If your game plan is to tell her what to buy based on features and price, then you need to rethink your strategy: **give her options for redesigning her life**

chapter 2

Jolt

"A lie can travel half way around the world while the truth is putting on its shoes."

—Mark Twain

Women weren't surprised about the economic downturn. With rarely an exception, the women we spoke with said they were aware that a downturn was likely. But what they hadn't bargained for was the **degree** to which their lives would be altered. More than 80 percent of the women we surveyed revealed that the Great Recession has had a negative impact on their lives. Based on our survey, that impact was particularly pronounced for women between the ages of 39 and 45, for Baby Boomers between the ages of 51 and 60, and for Caucasian women. Clearly, the severity and duration of the Great Recession was an unwelcome jolt that many women hadn't anticipated.

UNWELCOMED JOLT

"The Great Recession has had a **negative impact** on my life":

80+ percent

"It was so fast and powerful," said Cindy Watkins, age 42, of Colorado. "We knew it was coming, but the impact was so much more severe than what we had planned for. My husband and I were just beginning to appreciate our hard work and making the kind of money that allowed us to live the kind of lifestyle we wanted. That ended pretty quickly."

creeping distrust

Janet Epps listened to the advice of others. She graduated from George Washington University with a degree in finance. She went on to earn a master's degree in marketing science from Atlanta University, finishing top in her class and graduated with a job as a product manager at Ralston-Purina in St. Louis. She worked her way up the ranks by advancing to higher-paying jobs with greater responsibility. After owning her vacation home for 15 years, at the age of 50, Janet handed the keys to the bank. "I feel duped," said Epps. "I did everything that people to be trusted said I needed to do. I went to good schools, worked in great companies. I made conservative investments in retirement accounts and real estate. On paper, everything was smart and logical. So when the economy began to get a little shaky in '06 and '07, I wasn't overly concerned. I'd seen economic downturns before—the technology bust and 9/11. When I look back, I still can't figure out how this happened. I'm intelligent and financially savvy. Was I wrong or misled?"

> "I feel duped. When I look back, I still can't figure out how this happened. I'm intelligent and financially savvy. **Was I wrong or misled?"**
>
> *Janet Epps*

Women like Janet Epps don't necessarily point to brands or retailers as the culprits or causes of the Great Recession, yet many women have lost varying degrees of trust in the institutions and people who were guiding society. As a result of the initial fallout of the Great Recession and the lengthy economic downturn, women have developed a kind of creeping distrust. This overall disillusionment and general distrust is permeating all kinds of relationships, including those she previously enjoyed with brands. Sixty-four percent of women in our online panel report they have lost trust in companies, institutions, and brands. The percentage jumps to 73 percent of women between the ages of 51 and 60 who report they've lost confidence. Trust issues are least exhibited by women of an Asian cultural background. What should concern marketers even more than female consumers' distrust in brands, is the distrust they feel in general. Our study reveals that a whopping 62 percent said that they have greater distrust in general. Again, that number jumps to 70 percent for women ages 51 through 60.

DISILLUSIONED?

Percent of women who say they have **lost confidence in companies, institutions and brands**

all women surveyed:
64 percent

women aged 51-60:
73 percent

Percent of women who say they have **greater distrust in general**

all women surveyed:
62 percent

women aged 51-60:
70 percent

Women, who are more time-strapped than ever, are finding it takes more time and additional information to assess choices, to filter out those companies they deem good and trustworthy, and those brands that deliver what they promise. As a marketer, if you believe your brand, even those that are iconic, is exempt from "distrust creep" then we urge you to think again. Women's overall distrust extends to products, services and businesses they have patronized in the past, even when they were loyal customers. One of the effects of distrust creep that we've identified is less tolerance that consumers have for any perceived mistakes or misdoings on the side of brands. She is much less forgiving than she's ever been, and it doesn't take much for a brand to fall out of favor for mistakes real or perceived.

In an excerpt from a talk that psychologist John Gottman, professor emeritus of psychology at the University of Washington and co-founder of the Gottman Relationship Institute, presented at the Greater Good Science Center, the prolific author and noted relationship expert pointed out that "Trust is one of the most commonly used words in the English language—it's number 949. When I went to Amazon.com and typed in "trust," I was surprised that 36,000 books came up."[1]

According to psychologists, when the bond of trust is broken it causes people to doubt their own judgment and become suspect of any goodness in the world. Women understand the overall sequence of events that caused the economic dominos to fall leading to the start of the Great Recession in 2007. Because they understand that sequence of events, their trust of the institutions and governing bodies with oversight of them was put on alert.

the shifting calculus of brand loyalty

So how does the trust vacuum impact brands? Three words: strained brand loyalty. The American Marketing Association defines brand loyalty as "The situation in which a consumer generally buys the same manufacturer-originated product or service repeatedly over time rather than buying from multiple suppliers within the category."[2]

The Great Recession shifted the calculus of brand loyalty as we know it. For the women we interviewed, loyalty today has little resemblance to the loyalty she might have shown to a brand prior to 2007. About a third of the women we surveyed (32 percent) said they were less loyal to companies today than before the Great Recession, with an almost equal number (31 percent) revealing they are less loyal to brands. For women between the ages of 46 and 50 the percentage of women who are less loyal to companies jumps to 44 percent, while 41 percent indicated they are less loyal to brands.

Of the multi-cultural groups we explored in our online panels, we found that Latinas reported the greatest degree of disloyalty to companies and brands as a result of the Great Recession. Forty-three percent of Hispanic women report they are less loyal to companies and forty-five percent say they are less loyal to brands, both since the onset of the economic downturn.

With trust in brands faltering and loyalty nose-diving, marketers will find it more of a challenge than ever to establish or maintain brand fidelity. The strategies and tactics that had been in place will need to be recycled and replaced with a mindset and approach that takes into account that today women are far more interested in a superb transaction that results in a relationship based on mutual respect rather than trust. To expect more from her at this time is likely asking more from her than she is willing to accommodate.

LESS LOYAL?

Percent of women who say they are **less loyal to companies**

all women surveyed:
32 percent

women aged 46-50:
44 percent

Latinas:
43 percent

Percent of women who say they are **less loyal to brands**

all women surveyed:
31 percent

women aged 46-50:
41 percent

Latinas:
45 percent

the transaction rules

In Marketing 101 courses on college campuses nationwide, students have been feasting on a healthy recipe for the strategies and tactics required to establish consumer loyalty: the Holy Grail. And before 2007, prior to the establishment opening the kimono full tilt so citizens could witness the unraveling of the economy, it was logical to focus marketing capital and resources on driving meaningful emotional connections between a brand and the consumer. The ultimate goal has been to create a loyal relationship between an entity and a human based on a variety of assets, including, but not limited to, attributes, value and aspirations. While there is a wealth of expert advice on customer service, little attention has been given to the importance of the transaction between women and brands—in whole or as a series of critical steps that comprise a transaction. Is the packaging appealing, easy to handle, and easy to understand? Is the

Today, women are far more interested in a **superb transaction** that results in a relationship based on **mutual respect** **rather than trust.**

brand presentation at retail eye-catching? Is customer service easy to engage and focused on solving problems? Does the product perform as promised? Does the consumer feel fulfilled because they can get a job done? Did the cashier smile and say "Thank you. Have a nice day?"

There is more science than ever to support the finding that 85 percent of all consumer decisions are based in the subconscious part of the brain.[3] And never before has there been a time when marketers need to tap that cerebral cortex. However, with the historic economic circumstances and the robust purchase information platforms, we see the consumer driving a shift from *relationship* to *transaction*. While this departure may be concerning, it need not be. Distrust, self-reported consumer disloyalty and technology have created an environment where the consumer craves easy transactions. Now, there is tangible long-term value in providing a consumer a flawless transaction.

creating good chemistry

We found an interesting way to think about trust and loyalty from a neuroscience perspective, and a reminder that trust is not just a fickle emotion. According to neuropsychologist Loretta Graziano Breuning, Ph.D, when humans trust someone, the brain releases oxytocin, a potent neurochemical that makes us feel happy. "Oxytocin wires your brain to seek opportunities to trust to get more of that safe feeling," she writes in *Psychology Today*. Dr. Breuning continues:

> "But when someone betrays our trust, the brain releases a different neurochemical, cortisol, which feels bad. Cortisol signals pain, and wires you to avoid whatever caused the pain. Everything associated with a betrayal of trust tends to trigger your cortisol alarm in the future. When you trust, you risk ending up with that unpleasant cortisol feeling. But when you withhold trust, you miss out on that pleasant oxytocin feeling. So in every moment you must choose whether you are better off trusting or withholding trust. It's a daunting task, but your brain evolved to do it."[4]

A woman may repeatedly purchase the same products, but a repeat purchase doesn't mean she is loyal to the brand. If anything, she is more discerning out of necessity. So while marketers are marching on to the beat of brand loyalty, seeking symbiotic relationships with consumers based on trust, she is skeptical. Her proverbial oxytocin coffers are empty. Her trust is eroded and in many cases she is incapable or unwilling to give you fidelity, which is why women are willing to gamble on an excellent transaction.

> A woman may repeatedly purchase the same products, but a repeat purchase **doesn't mean she is loyal to the brand.**

One member of a group of 40-something friends who live in the same neighborhood in a middle-class subdivision in the northern suburbs of Atlanta described the group's take on brand loyalty.

"We all shop differently now.
We're aware of how the
system works."
Kim Gonano

"We all shop differently now," said Kim Gonano, age 45. "We're aware of how the system works. There are two grocery stores about the same distance from our homes. We know we can save more money at one and they have a wide selection. The other, Publix, tends to be a little more expensive. But we all try to shop there as much as possible because we know what to expect from them—from the lighting in the parking lot to the bag boy helping with the groceries. We know what they're about every step of the shopping trip," Gonano said. "They support the community, their service is excellent and the environment is pleasing. They showed up at my neighbor's home, right after Hurricane Katrina. She ended up providing temporary housing to half a dozen family members who'd lost everything to the storm. Publix brought groceries to her home because they'd heard about the situation from other customers. They are consistent—you never guess about what they stand for."

the relationship of excellent transactions

Buyology, Inc. is a consulting firm dedicated to helping clients structure, interpret, and execute solutions that measure and leverage nonconscious decision making. The firm uses a technique called "latency response," in which research participants must choose a response quickly before conscious thought takes over. The brands that made the firm's "Most Desired Brands in the U.S." list for 2012 are examples of strategic templates for success in building a relationship with women through excellent transactions: Southwest Airlines, Dove, and Hallmark are a few examples.[5]

These brands appeal to women because they are:

- **authentic** – *she knows what they stand for,*
- **dependable** – *she can count on the product or service and the purchase experience,*
- **empathetic** – *they get where she is coming from,*
- have a **strong orientation for customer experience** – *fast, easy, even fun,*
- and are, of course, a **good value** – *worth the price in dollars and in time.*[5]

As a marketer, think of the relationship vs. transaction mindset as the sequence of steps involved in a budding romantic relationship between a brand and someone you like very much, someone who controls 85 percent of consumer purchase decisions.[6] There is a first date. If both people get along and are compatible and the experience is pleasant, they will move on to a second date, and she will start to talk about the quality of the interaction with friends. It usually takes a lot of independent encounters to form a relationship. Without those independent encounters, or transactions, there's no long-term relationship.

> Consumers will bet on these kinds of brands in the post recession:
> Authentic
> Dependable
> Empathetic
> Good customer experience
> Good value

We encourage clients to alter their thinking and focus on building a platform for a series of excellent transactions. Amazon is a good example of a brand that not only provides a variety of options for product purchases—new and used—but makes the purchase transaction (and return option) simple. Amazon uses a

> Build a platform for **a series of excellent transactions.**

variety of techniques and technology solutions to better understand the needs of their customers in ways that foster opportunities to communicate special deals on favorite products and suggest affinity products. Even the Amazon smiley face box signals that she's made a good choice. Her oxytocin starts to regenerate.

What does she want from the transaction? Keep your promises and remain consistent. Don't surprise her. Demonstrate why your product pricing is fair and make the transaction simple.

Chapter 3

Hustle

C arol Jones had never been a coupon-clipper. Far from it. Researching the discounts from the neighborhood super-market, clipping coupons, and sorting them took too much time. And when she did remember to use the ones she'd tossed in the bottom of her handbag, they were typically past the redemption date. But that all changed when the Great Recession rolled in. "I don't have a choice now," said the 45-year-old mother of three teenage sons. "My husband and I both work, and though neither of us lost our jobs, we did lose about 40 percent of our take home pay. If I don't take time to hunt down the bargains, we can't make ends meet. That's not an option with three hungry growing boys in the house."

How much of "the deal" takes place on **computers** and **mobile devices**?

2012: $186.2 billion

▲ **5% from 2011**

the daily action

While the days of browsing the Sunday circulars for grocery savings are far from extinct, the real action for the "the deal" is taking place on computers and mobile devices, to the tune of $186.2 billion in 2012 (up 5 percent from 2011)[1] in homes across the country. Dear

Marketer, from the women who control $5 trillion in consumer spending, Game On![2] Out of a genuine necessity and with a gatherer's mentality in our DNA, women are maneuvering and managing a sophisticated portfolio of daily deals, couponing platforms, and consumer reviews to balance tight household and personal budgets. Discounts, half-off pricing, buy-one-get-one-free offers, and the like are delivered on the hour straight to her in-box or her smartphone from a wide range of daily deal sites.

From its launch as an off-shoot of a website called The Point in 2008, Groupon is now the largest of the daily deals offerings and is traded on Nasdaq (GRPN). With 35 million registered users, Groupon serves 150 markets in North America (and at least 100 more around the world).[3] Groupon, its closest competitor LivingSocial, and the hundreds of copycat sites, understand that the Carol Jones' of the world want a deal. They serve as a broker between a product, service, or brand and the consumer, helping to draw the subscriber in with an excellent offering and a deeply discounted price.

According to Groupon, the brand-consumer matchmaking benefits the customer companies by introducing them to a viable audience and inspiring a transaction. According to the company's website, the founders:

". . . came up with the idea for Groupon as an antidote to a common ailment for us city-dwellers: there's so much cool stuff to do, but the choice can be overwhelming. With so many options, sometimes the easiest thing is to go to a familiar restaurant, or just stay at home and watch a movie. As a result, we miss out on trying all the cool things our cities have to offer. Groupon makes it simple by offering only the best businesses in your area. And by leveraging The Point's framework for collective buying, Groupon is able to offer deals that make it very difficult to say no. While we started Groupon as a side project of The Point, it's taken on a life of its own."[4]

masters of the age of the deal

For the women who leverage services like Groupon, the art of the deal is becoming increasingly more straightforward and savings are realized more quickly. Combined with discounts directly from retailers—both brick-and-mortar and online sites—women have emerged as the masters of the deal. And they will tell you that the deal has to be great or it's insulting. So who is hustling whom?

The flip side to the abundance of opportunities for women to purchase goods and services at a discount is that in the rush to drive purchase, marketers may have overlooked an important element in the consumer-brand relationship and consumer behavior. The constant drive to push trial has created an expectation among women that they will never have to pay full price for a product they are willing to try or re-buy. If there is not a deal available to them at the time they are ready to make the purchase, they'll wait it out. Or worse, they'll product hop to execute the transaction elsewhere or experiment with another brand. "I probably get 20 emails a day between those from the big guys and from the local deal companies offering everything from half-off Botox to buy-one-get-one-free dinners," says Tania Walters. "When they offer a really good deal on something I know I like or for a service I want to try, then they get my attention. If I have a great experience, I might try it again and I usually tell

> Women expect to **never have to pay full price for a product again.** If no deal is available now, **they'll wait it out or product hop.**

my friends or co-workers about it. But the companies should never assume they have me in their pockets. If another deal comes along that I think is better or for a particular brand I want to try, then I'll jump." One of the consequences for the daily deal offer is that it can erode loyalty between a brand and the consumer. The better offerings achieve traffic spikes and may increase loyalty to the deal site rather than the product or service being offered. And more daily deals aren't necessarily better.

Few product categories are exempt from "The Hustle." Women have greater access to product information, comparative data on price and quality, and even the sponsoring company's investor information. And as a result, they have real transparency into pricing strategies, and the back-of-the-house merchandising and retailing strategies. This trend toward info-loading is not limited to the mainstream, middle-market shopper. "All shoppers, including the luxury shoppers, are smarter, more informed and more discerning about a purchase," says Alf Nucifora, chairman and founder of the Luxury Marketing Council of San Francisco, Monterey Peninsula, and Las Vegas. "The power has migrated from the marketer to the consumer, who in some cases had been taken advantage of for a long time."

> Shoppers are smarter, more informed and more discerning about a purchase. **Power has migrated from the marketer to the consumer.**

Consumer marketing expert Melissa Murphy, who has worked in senior corporate communications positions in both consulting firms and in top-tier consumer goods companies Del Monte and StarKist, says that "women are putting brands and retailers on notice. Your customer wants the best deal that you have to offer and nothing less will do." Driven by the proliferation of deals and out of a necessity to economize, women concede that they have been paying inflated prices for everything from barbecue to Botox. With the promise of a great deal just for insiders, online sites like Rue La La and One Kings Lane borrowed a page from members-only warehouse clubs, like Costco or Sam's Club, and opened up their virtual kimono to offer high-end merchandise for a fraction of the cost and only to those in on the secret.

rewards of insider trading

One of the assets of the deal-oriented exchange between brand and consumer is that warm and fuzzy feeling a consumer gets when she's part of the inside circle. She becomes an insider who has information, advance knowledge, and direct access to products before the rest of the buying public. Consumers, regardless of the amount of discretionary spending available to them, want the members-only treatment. Warehouse buying clubs recognized the value of this "insider" mentality long ago. Rue La La characterizes itself as an exclusive, invitation-only destination where members discover premier brand, private sale boutiques, each open for just a short time. Its focus is a "well-edited collection of sought-after offerings from the best brand names in the world. Access to products previously unattainable for many consumers, combined with helpful service, has contributed to the popularity and prosperity of Rue La La's founders."[5] Gilt.com provides instant insider access to today's top designer labels, at up to 60 percent off retail. One Kings Lane, the brainchild of two female entrepreneurs, went live in 2009 during the height of the Recession. With a slightly different offering than Gilt.com or Rue La La, One Kings Lane is focused on the home furnishings, accessories, and décor category by offering a range of products during a "sale" that lasts 72 hours. Along with Zulily.com, a similar online site that features daily sales of products for moms, babies, and kids, the members-only exchanges are successfully tapping into an expectant woman or mom's need to feel valued. As a result, Zulily.com is building a loyal following of subscribers who have a propensity to spend on products for their offspring.

But what is happening to the aspiration marketers so often want to create between consumers and a high-end brand? In our research, we have learned that women are in an emotional struggle between the satisfaction of getting a great high-end product at a fraction of the cost and the disillusionment from recognizing that they've been overspending on that product in the past. With a type of black currency booming, women's loyalty is proving to be more fickle than ever. As the deals swell in their in-boxes and on their mobile phones, so does the sense that retailers and brands have been fooling them. So women are meeting that head-on with the power of mobile devices and working their own deals.

The days of the Saturday afternoon family road trip to personally shop three appliance stores for a new refrigerator may be gone, but the number of channels used for the shopping experience has exploded. Don't assume for a minute that only one channel of information will be enough to keep your brand and your product as part of a decision set for today's consumer. She has all the channels at her fingertips—online, mobile, floor sales, and personal recommendations—and she still accesses at least three different options prior to purchase.[6] The need for meticulous integrated marketing and channel management have never been as important as today.

keeping it in the family

The average household belongs to 18 consumer loyalty programs and the programs are active in almost half of the homes.[7] The idea behind a loyalty program is to keep a consumer comfortable in the bosom of a brand by rewarding her for spending her dollars with your brand or in your store. The traditional loyalty program where a consumer needs to have a stock-paper card punched or swipe a plastic card is going out the window, replaced by programs that understand loyalty is about solving a problem and enticing her with something she really wants and can relish. Quick-serve restaurant Panera Bread understands that consumers want tangible proof that the rewards are accumulating toward a meaningful payoff. In the My Panera program, patrons are rewarded after one transaction with a free pastry and points are tracked automatically at the cash register. Staples sends coupons to members' in-boxes weekly, with significant savings on everyday products and meaningful reductions for bigger ticket items. Cosmetics store Sephora rewards members with trial-size products available in stores and certificates for special birthday bonuses.

While gifts and perks are enticing, appreciated and help keep them engaged, women are regularly searching for companies and products that bring them solutions. With such a rich data profile available, smart loyalty programs will not only make the process easy with regular paybacks and communication, they can also find more ways to engage consumers by delivering customized content that addresses their Great Recession-driven needs and the value proposition of a brand. From advice on the hot colors and fashion tips for redheads in spring, to tips for hosting a better office lunch meeting from a nearby sandwich shop, now more than ever,

> While gifts and perks are enticing, appreciated and help keep her engaged, women are **regularly searching for companies and products to bring her solutions.** Smart loyalty programs not only make the process easy with regular paybacks and communication, they also engage by delivering **customized content.**

women are evaluating their preference for companies and brands with a longer list of criteria that is rich in solutions.

The Hustle Economy

In 2010, *Time* magazine referred to the current economic state as the Sheconomy, a term quickly adopted and used to describe the spending power and influence of female purchasers.[8] As individuals and as a collective, women are responsible for $5 trillion spending annually and are gatekeepers for many of the purchases at home and in the workplace.[9] What the Sheconomy doesn't recognize is the system women use to obtain goods and services and the nature by which they are trading resources. We have learned that women don't define the economy as an exchange of currency. It isn't content for Sunday morning political programming, nor a metric that reflects the fiscal health of the nation or global marketplace. For the majority of women we researched, the economy is a personal indicator about the health of her household, her family, and her personal life. Her opinion of the economy is heavily cloaked in the sacrifices and changes that she has experienced, and as a result, how she has reorganized her life, including where she shops, how she shops, even how she prepares to make a purchase. In fact, one form of the word "economy" is derived from the Greek "oikonomos," meaning household manager.

> A women's own economic condition can be marked by how **knowledgeable, adept and clever** she is at **organizing, planning for and negotiating purchases** to maximize time and wring out the greatest value for the least cost. We call this **the Hustle Economy**.

A woman's economy is complex and dynamic. Her opinion of her own economic condition can be marked by how knowledgeable, adept, and clever she is at organizing, planning for, and negotiating purchases to maximize time and wring out the greatest value for the least cost. We call this the Hustle Economy. There is good news for brands doing business with women in a Hustle Economy. The opportunity to differentiate yourself is robust and straightforward. There aren't necessarily new strategies but core techniques that need to be executed well and delivered consistently. Be mindful that women are operating in the Age of the Deal, which represents both a game and a high-stakes financial exercise. Unless your brand has never offered a discount, a coupon, a savings reward, or an outlet store, her expectation is that you have a deal for her or will soon.

core techniques executed well, delivered consistently

Von Maur department stores aren't the least expensive game in town, but for shoppers familiar with this Midwestern-based department store, it is the real deal. Von Maur, a family owned retailer out of Iowa, is a throw back in time, offering shoppers free gift wrap, free shipping, and an interest-free charge account. The company invests in its sales associates and expects them to use that training to build clientele. Combined with excellent customer service and a manageable selection of mid to higher-end products, the retailer is actually expanding into new markets in countertrend to the new retail landscape. To reinforce its commitment to the retro, quality retail experience, it remains committed to keeping the lobby pianist for the customer's shopping pleasure.

Neither a mainstream chain nor a dollar store, grocery retailer Aldi has found its niche. By catering to the cost-conscious shopper through low prices on highly rated private label goods that are comparable to name brands, Aldi has a distinctive model that consumers find appealing. The stores are meticulous, well-lit, and the commodity packaging is appealing. The chain gives deep discounts to shoppers who don't need frills and a pleasing environment. Shoppers pay a twenty-five cent deposit to use a shopping cart, they bag their own groceries with bags from home, and pay with cash, debit cards, or check. No old-fashioned, cluttered, dirty discount store, Aldi has found a way to help frugal consumers stock their pantries at a great value. And don't be surprised to see a Range Rover next to a sub-compact in the parking lot; Aldi appeals to affluent shoppers as well as the most budget-conscious of consumers.

In today's game, the table stakes are straight-forward, but not always easy to implement. Remember women are looking for help and stability, so demonstrate how you are supporting them during tough times. Remain consistent in your message and communicate it clearly, frequently and across multiple platforms. Melissa Murphy reminds us that "If a consumer doesn't hear from you for a while, she doesn't know what you've been doing and may have moved on to another alternative." Interestingly, almost six percent of loyalty club members say they never hear a peep from the brand they engaged after the day they signed up.[10]

The interaction between consumer and brand and more importantly, the deal, has to be transparent and easy for her to understand and manage. More bells and whistles or steps required to get a reward do not advance the cause. While The Hustle might be considered the game she is playing as she works the deal, it also harkens back to the 1980s disco era. The Hustle, with choreography danced to four/four music while counted in triple time, was no simple move. As the post Great Recession woman spins to this complex syncopation, smart marketers will figure out how to re-define their consumer partnership and take on enough flexibility so that she feels she can lead the dance.

Chapter 4

Escape Hatches

Women have long been considered the gender most likely to commit—the fairer sex looking for the stability and permanence of a committed relationship in which we could direct our innate desire to nurture and bond. Prior to 2007, in our consulting work, we showed clients the similarities between the typical architecture of a relationship between two adults and that of an adult and a brand:

Stage one: Infatuation

Dear Mascara, my eyes are brilliant and my lashes reach to the moon.

Stage two: Disillusionment

Dear Mascara, my eyelashes don't look long and there are clumps.

Stage three: Mutual Accommodation

Dear Mascara, maybe the clumps are there because I've had this tube of mascara for six months. Brand Big Lash, I'll give you another shot.

According to psychologist Robert Simmermon, co-founder of The Haystack Group and gifted counseling psychologist, many relationships fail because one or both of the parties have trouble navigating Stage Two (disillusionment), even though it is a natural step in the progression of any relationship. "It isn't realistic to believe any healthy relationship will remain permanently in the infatuation stage," says Simmermon. The key, he says, is to learn how to jockey between Stages Two and Three. That is where the committed relationship lives.

no strings, please

What we've found in our research of women in the Great Recession era is that while our innate tendency is to seek and form relationships that provide structure and permanence, the reality is that women are now shying away from that type of commitment. They are looking for escape hatches in everyday interactions, from signing estimates for a contractor and long-term contracts with a cell phone carrier, to backing away from regularly scheduled housekeeping appointments and community service positions. No strings attached, please. The women we talked with are looking to create opportunities to quickly exit a relationship or scenario that they feel are boxing them in and to extend their runways to buy time in order to scope out and consider all of their options and delay decision-making.

> Women in the Great Recession era are shying from commitment. They are looking for **escape hatches** in everyday interactions.

The challenge for marketers is working to move consumers to a committed relationship of mutual respect and accommodation, when women in the post-recessionary era are brand-hopping, moving on to greener pastures before they even become disillusioned by a brand, product, service or retailer. Prior to the Great Recession, smart brands planned ahead for the natural rhythm of the consumer-brand relationship and had plans in place to maintain fidelity in spite of a natural tendency to stray after a few bumps in the road. Starbucks has done a brilliant job of maintaining strong relationships with their female patrons by engaging them in the solutions to help alleviate churn from Stage Two's disillusionment. With hundreds of beverage variations offered—there's even a WikiHow post on how to order at Starbucks so one doesn't slow down the process for other customers in line—the chain keeps consumers in the fold with helpful new products and extensions. Tired of coffee? Try Tazo tea. Want to stay awhile? Enjoy complimentary in-store WiFi. Hungry while you work? Select from a line of pre-packaged eats. Taking a break? Here's a card with a redemption code for a free iTunes download. Whether you like the coffee or not, Starbucks has a compelling model that keeps you engaged and less inclined to consider alternative competitors. In comparison, an Atlanta Bread Company store down the street requires patrons to purchase a food or drink item before they will reveal the WiFi code printed on a receipt. In a time when even the local grocery story has WiFi, this is an outdated and potentially lethal practice.

> Women are embracing the adage of "Keep your options open" and looking for **flexibility** that allows her a **choice**: stay put, move on, or make no decision at all.

How many times have we heard the advice, "Keep your options open?" Women are embracing this adage and looking for flexibility that allows them a choice: stay put, move on, or make no decision at all.

But what's wrong with wanting an escape hatch or a longer runway? Dr. Heidi Grant Halvorson believes that keeping options open is a really bad idea. A social psychologist and the author of *The Psychology of Goals*, Dr. Halvorson has an insightful take on the wisdom of the sages. In *Psychology Today* she writes,

> "People overwhelmingly prefer reversible decisions to irreversible ones. They believe it's better to 'keep your options open,' whenever possible. They wait years before declaring a major, date someone for years before getting married, favor stores with a guaranteed return policy (think Zappos), and hire employees on a temporary basis, all in order to avoid commitments that can be difficult, or nearly impossible, to undo. People believe that this is the best way to ensure their own happiness and success. But people, as it turns out, are wrong."[1]

Research by Dan Gilbert, a Harvard psychologist and author of *Stumbling on Happiness* (Vintage, 2007), shows that decisions that are reversible tend to lead to lower levels of satisfaction than irreversible decisions. Dr. Gilbert believes that once someone makes a final decision, the psychological immune system kicks in, which is how our minds have the ability to make us feel positive about our decisions. "Once we've committed to a course of action, we stop thinking about alternatives, or we conclude the decision we make is superior to ones we didn't choose,"[2] Gilbert says. Dr. Halvorson concludes that when we keep options open, we continue to think about the alternatives.

*reversible decisions tend to lead to **lower levels of satisfaction***

Not only are we distracted by the intellectual see-saw, but our psychological immune system isn't triggered and as a result, we feel less happy.

Gregory Berns, author of *Iconoclast*, (Harvard Business Press, 2008) theorizes that fear causes us to be hyper-vigilant and impairs our decision-making. "Fear prompts retreat. It is the antipode to progress. Just when we need new ideas most, everyone is seized up in fear, trying to prevent losing what we have left," says the Emory University neuroscientist.[3]

Almost three out of four women (74 percent) in our survey revealed that they are slower to make a decision in the era of the Recession than pre-2007. That number creeps up to 80 percent for Asian women and 79 percent for women between the ages of 46 and 50. Women explain that in making purchase decisions today, they have to be more thoughtful, more informed, and base their choice on more research than ever before. With reduced household budgets, many explain that unless the purchase is tied to an immediate or critical need, they might just be avoiding the reality and, perhaps, the permanence of a new purchase.

CHOOSIER?

Percent of women who say they are **slower to make a decision**

all women surveyed:
74 percent

women aged 46-50:
46 percent

Asian women:
80 percent

the good news

So for marketers, there's good news and there's bad news. The good news first: the options for providing her with the tools for decision making have never been more prolific and the costs never more economical. Social media platforms like Facebook (845 million users), YouTube (484 million users) and Twitter (20 million users) have nominal costs of entry and provide advertisers with faster, more interactive and data-driven media placement than ever before. Brands can react quickly, retract quickly, and distribute their content with a fraction of the media and production cost of televi-

Tools for decision making have never been **more prolific** and the costs never **more economical.**

sion, newspaper, and print and with greater variety of photos, text, video, or music.

You have the opportunity not to just sell to her but to solve problems for her by sharing solution-oriented content, entertainment, and rewards—24/7 from any location and with lightning speed.

the bad news

Now the bad news: The management and integration of that content is critical as she shops multiple channels and reviews sites to gain confidence in her decision—increasingly from a sales-room floor. The process tends to be far more complicated, requiring constant calibration. The greatest of communications will be quickly clicked over if the user experience is unfriendly or complex. Don't make the options so numerous, overwhelming or irrelevant that she cannot make up her mind. And know that if your product or brand doesn't remain front and center in her life, she will begin to forget the connection or meaning it once held. Her new, edited, yet information-driven lifestyle leaves room for only so many considerations.

> Managing and integrating content is critical as she shops multiple channels and review sites to gain **confidence** in her decision.

By protracting the decision to make a purchase and extending the sales cycle, women have upped the ante for brands. Of the women we surveyed, 64 percent already believe that advertisers do not understand their needs today, an opinion even more pronounced for women over age 50 and Latina shoppers, both 68 percent. Implementing a strategy and creative execution that introduces her to a new brand or reinforces that she has made the right purchase decision with an existing brand is a straightforward way to stand out in a crowded field.

- Make the transaction with your brand fun, easy, stress-free, and rewarding.

- Allow her the opportunity to ask questions and respond quickly with information that feeds her curiosity and intelligence.

- Demonstrate the value compared to the price.

- And above all, for commodity categories or those overcrowded with options, practice patience and message consistency.

UNDERSTANDING?

Percent of women who say "**advertisers don't understand my needs**"

all women surveyed: 64 percent

women over 50 and Latinas: 68 percent

Brands frequently mentioned by the women we surveyed have several things in common that women see as ways the brands are anticipating her needs in this difficult economic environment.

- First, they offer discounts or sales.

- Two, they provide useful information and tips or shortcuts for getting things accomplished, like making a meal.

- Three, the products work well or the service is excellent.

- Four, there is a money-back guarantee and easily accessed customer service.

Brands most often cited in unaided responses among women we surveyed include Kellogg's, Honda, Tide, Apple, Amazon, Aldi, Walmart, McDonald's, Costco, Target, and Procter & Gamble. One of the most interesting stories we discovered was from a woman in Arizona who gave the example of a dry cleaner in her area offering free dry cleaning for area residents interviewing for jobs.

Jackie Bird, CEO of the Red Bean Society, is an expert in marketing to the Latina shopper. In describing the mindset of the Latina in the post-Recession period, she reminds us that the values of family, home, and culture are important and that brands that communicate their importance to Latinas—beyond just a low price—have an opportunity to gain a foothold with this powerful consumer segment.

500 channels

A stroll down the frozen desserts aisle of a typical supermarket could net a shopper more than a dozen brands and more than 40 product names of ice cream, frozen yogurts, sorbets and ice-cream related treats, in all representing around 360 choices. Does the American family need hundreds of frozen dessert choices? In the early days of The Haystack Group, we began exploring a hypothetical "true north" for every consumer, the one necessity universal to all human beings in a position to purchase. This need had to be one that could be met by brands and would form a lasting imprint on the consumer. Thanks to Dr. Simmermon, we honed in on the power of potential. Every consumer, from cradle to grave needs to feel they are achieving an effect, making progress. While our potential can be enhanced through making new discoveries, having to choose a quart of ice cream doesn't count. It's difficult to achieve an intended effect, like getting in and out of the grocery store quickly and within budget, when we're faced with an overwhelming array of options.

> Her edited lifestyle leaves room for only so many considerations. Don't make the options so numerous, overwhelming or irrelevant that **she cannot make up her mind.**

In *The Paradox of Choice: Why More is Less* (Harper Perennial, 2005), Barry Schwartz explains why we are overwhelmed when confronted with the array of choices in the cold and cough aisle at a neighborhood drug store. Like staring down a rabbit hole, too many choices can lead to decision-making impotence. In the book's description, we are counseled that "choice overload can make you question the decisions you make before you even make them, it can set you up for unrealistically high expectations, and it can make you blame yourself for any and all failures."

The key to success for marketers and brand managers is to have an intimate understanding of how your female consumer sees increased value in your brand—not solely in terms of what your product or service has to offer—but rather the context of it in her life and how flexible you are about her ability to engage, then disengage, and engage yet again. She sees this as your willingness to acknowledge her need for an escape hatch. It's hard not to be offended at the notion a consumer isn't interested in a relationship with your brand. Some day she may be, but like many bonds, she'll have to get there in her own time, as she becomes more practiced at working Stages Two and Three of the relationship. Stay the course and stay closely in touch with how her definition of value evolves during the next three years. And be okay with the idea of a transactional relationship. If you string together enough high quality transactions, over time you will have a loyal purchaser or consumer. She just isn't comfortable with the return to commitment yet.

chapter 5

Trading Down

Every year, in Buddhist temples across Japan, bells are rung 108 times to welcome the New Year. The tolling of temple bells at midnight is a way to shed evil passions and purify followers for the upcoming year. The ceremony, called *Joya no Kane*, recognizes the Buddhist belief that 108 is a sacred number, representing the number of passions and desires that entrap people in a cycle of suffering and reincarnation. The 108 bell chimes symbolize the purification from the same number of delusions and sufferings accumulated in the past year.

Women we've talked with are re-engineering their lives through their own forms of *Joya no Kane*, casting off objects, ideas, and even relationships that weigh them down. In this movement we call "Editing Life," women are saying good-bye to household items, furniture and clothing, severing ties with companies and brands and even relinquishing personal relationships, all with the singular goal of shaking loose things or people who aren't a positive influence or don't deliver either short-term or lasting value. Francine Jay is a minimalist, author, and popular blogger whose insights are posted

> Women are re-engineering their lives —editing out objects, ideas, and even relationships that weigh them down.

regularly on her blog, MissMinimalist.com. Jay sees the minimalist trend—which she calls the "minsumer" movement—growing by leaps and bounds as women in particular look to shed negative emotions, expressions and tangibles. While the women we spoke with may not declare themselves official card-carrying members of the minimalist union, they are increasingly de-cluttering their closets and their psyches in a way that is important to marketers.[1]

less is . . . freeing?

In the heydays prior to the economic meltdown, many women were in acquisition mode. Ultimately finding there was too much to balance and too many conflicting needs to manage, their reaction to the stress and burden of the Great Recession has been to edit their lives by shedding anything that doesn't provide value or represent a potentially fruitful investment. Women are flocking to the "less is more club," where acquiring a new attitude has replaced acquiring a new handbag. The same is true of relationships. With many people and needs tugging at them, women tell us they don't really have the time to properly maintain non-critical relationships and friendships. "I have a pretty wide network of friends and associates. And I found that I didn't really have the luxury of face time with anyone except close friends, so now I keep up with people through Facebook. I made the conscious choice to exit superficial relationships and focus only on those that are personal and meaningful or necessary to my job," said Sarah Wood, age 42. Perhaps women today are channeling Albert Einstein, whose three rules of work are:

- Out of clutter, find simplicity.
- From discord, find harmony.
- In the middle of difficulty lies opportunity.

According to Robert Simmermon, this behavior is one way people streamline the things in their lives they have to manage or care for. "Decluttering your physical and psychic environments is beneficial on many fronts—you have less to be responsible for, whether it's an unused treadmill taking up space in a basement or mismatched teacups—and the act of removing these unused things is very freeing on an emotional level," he says. "When we shed things that burden us or connect us with a negative emotion, it can be a cathartic step and free up space in our head to focus on taking positive steps."

"Decluttering your physical and psychic environments are beneficial on many fronts."

Dr. Robert Simmermon

"I sort of got to the point of being tired of feeling overwhelmed," said Melanie DeFleur of New Orleans. "I wanted to feel productive, like I was contributing in some way so I cleaned out a few closets and ended up with a big bag of things I drove to a second-hand store. It was great. I felt good about having less stuff in my house and I made a few dollars. I felt I had accomplished something." The popularity of consignment stores—from children's apparel to furniture and decorative arts—has risen to such a celebrity-like status that in many cities, day-long bus tours are being organized to deliver consumers to the front door step of participating retailers. "I grew up going to consignment and thrift stores with my grandmother. She had a very intentional routine—this store for housewares, that store for clothing. It made a tremendous impression on me," said Elizabeth Rasberry, a skilled consignment shopper. "I had a child in 2009 when the economy was taking a dive and quickly realized that those cute baby outfits are very expensive and not practical at all. I consigned most of his clothes and toys and still find the majority of his clothes at consignment stores."

less is . . . hip?

Before the Recession, talk about financial sacrifices was conducted in hushed tones. Like the way society used to talk about someone with cancer as having "the big C," people who encountered bankruptcy, foreclosure, or a similarly harsh financial crisis had a "little problem with money." It wasn't talked about. The Great Recession opened up conversations about household finances—ours or our neighbors'—and brought the discussion out into the open. And as painful as that was for a period of time, consumers found strength in numbers. Families and individuals facing economic hardships were not unique, but part of a swelling community that found comfort in the discussion becoming public and widespread.

As a result, one of the silver linings of our down economy was a rise in the free and engaging dialogue about the "coolness" of sacrifice, how smart we are for doing our homework and legwork and paying less. How being consumer savvy is the new state of prestige. Only the uninformed and out of it would continue to buy anything without a discount. With a morning dose of Clark Howard, consumer expert and host of nationally syndicated *The Clark Howard Show* radio show and co-host of HLN's nightly *Evening Express* television program, or daily tips and offers from Bradsdeals.com, or a variety of apps on their smart phone, women have the ability to trade down and trade smart. The marketplace helped reposition a negative mindset into messages about how smart the consumer is, how fun it is to be savvy, and what the value associated with it is. "There is a return to the historic norm of frugality and common sense," says Brad Wilson,

> One of the silver linings was the rise in the free and engaging dialogue about the "coolness" of **sacrifice**. Being consumer savvy is the new state of **prestige.**

founder of Bradsdeals.com, which is a one-stop online source for coupons, information, and links to good deals from leading retailers. "The psychology of consumers has changed dramatically; you could see it happen. We went from feeling we were losing in the retail marketplace and not knowing how, to understanding the game. Now we know why, and consumers have become very competitive so that they don't lose in any transaction."

less is . . . healthier?

Consumers are trading down beyond the boundaries of the retail setting into their homes, the workplace, and even doctor's offices. And the benefits exceed savings at a cash register. For example, women are returning to the kitchen to oversee homecooked meals as a strategy to manage budget-conscious households, and families are finding themselves together around the dinner table. The American Dietetic Association Foundation reported a dramatic increase in the number of daily family meals eaten at home, up from 52 percent in 2003 to 73 percent in 2010.[2]

meals eaten
at home

2010: 73%

▲ 21% since 2003

Discretionary dollars that had been funneled into molding kids into soccer superstars or academic champions dried up. As a result, children across America are finding they once again are normal. "We always provided opportunities for our kids that would help them advance and to achieve," said Gloria Cane of Michigan. "Finally, we weren't able to continue funding the private coaching, the music lessons, or the travel expenses for club sports. We were surprised at the family reaction. We thought everyone would be distraught, and feel neglected. After the initial adjustment, we discovered that neither the kids nor the parents needed all those extras to excel. In some ways, life is a lot easier now."

less is . . . easier?

We've learned that often, with acquisition, the cost is more than just the purchase price of the product. Maintenance costs, storage expenses, and insurance premiums—all add up to paperwork, unproductive dollars supporting the acquisition of something that wasn't all that important to begin with. As an example, the median cost of ownership for a midsized SUV over the first five years runs more than $9,100 a year, which makes the base model MINI Cooper a smart purchase beyond the "hip, cool" attitude of the car. In comparison, the annual cost to own a MINI Cooper is $5,800.[3] And, according to MiniUSA, the MINI is a car you can design more than 10 million different ways,[4] "so have a little fun creating a MINI to your exact specifications." High fuel costs and heightened ecological sensibilities have already steered families toward automotive options with improved fuel economy and fewer luxury ornaments on the hood. Even Jaguar, the storied automotive manufacturer, bid adieu to the multi-dimensional perched silver feline, replacing it with a two-dimensional medallion. The six-year trade in plan extended to eight, and eventually we were surprised to feel smart about owning a 10-year-old car. The average age of a car on the road today is 11-plus years, bringing renewed opportunity to car repair shops and automotive after market.[5]

Open a closet in the American home today and you'll see that

annual cost of owning:

SUV: $9,100

MINI: $5,800

age of the average US car

11+ years

American women are paring down wardrobes, cleaning out drawers in a quest to hone in on those items that are **high-quality, in good repair and have staying power.**

storage is king. Aligned with the trading down movement, women are substituting old shoe boxes, plastic containers and the like for trendy, fashionable mixed material storage solutions. Borrowing a page from the European philosophy on stuff, American women are paring down wardrobes, cleaning out drawers in a quest to hone in on those items that are high-quality, in good repair, and have staying power. Meredith Garcia, a fashion industry insider and co-founder of TheFashionList.com, sees the trend toward less is more on runways everywhere. She says:

> "I think big picture that the American sportswear category has changed. Since 2008, designers are putting out collections in blacks, white and cream. Women aren't buying full collections, but items with a longer shelf life. They accessorize with belts or timepieces with a pop of color."

In a trend mirroring the Depression, lipstick sales are up during the Recession.[6] After all, it's a cheap and easy way to perk up the pout.

"Now I get things altered. I have my good shoes resoled. I gave away my panini maker," says Sandy Simons of Texas. "I enjoy and appreciate well-made products and appreciate their lasting potential. My criteria are pretty simple—something has to be well-made, it has to serve multiple purposes, or it has to get the job done well. It may not be cool, but I'll hang on to my Crock-Pot until it dies." It's no wonder a Better Homes & Gardens slow cooker recipe book is one of the bestselling cookbooks on TheGoodCook.com.[7]

A commitment to less-specialized products, and more that were multipurpose, encouraged furniture and home décor producers to think about how to create products that could be a desk, an arts and crafts work station, and dining table all in one. We're even trading down on the names of the retailers, exchanging beautiful showrooms and fancy names for warehouse stores like The Dump. Wine consumption rose with the iconic "Two Buck Chuck" at Trader Joe's, which became "Three Buck Chuck" in early 2013, sold by the case to women who previously turned their noses up at it. "I'm always interested to see the kinds of wine that are being served now at parties. Women have learned that cheap can equal good. Costco appetizers, plucked from a warehouse, are not only served, but proudly promoted. Open that bag of shrimp, thaw it out, save $20, and brag about it.

less is . . . hands-on?

The prohibitive cost of renovation, along with the need to upgrade and maintain, have helped fuel DIY sales at home improvement stores around the country with 40 percent of power tools now being bought by women.[8] A Home Depot store in suburban Atlanta fosters these sales with seminars and training, and the company features women involved in DIY projects in its advertising. The gateway product is the battery-powered screwdriver and it takes off from there. While wall paper and paint were the areas of DIY expertise for women in the past, women now tile entire bathrooms or build out closets. "I was originally annoyed that I couldn't afford to hire this out, but now I am enjoying it. It makes me feel smart and in control," said Pennsylvania resident LaShanda Phillips.

The Recession has pushed DIY into other arenas previously left to experts. From hair color to automotive tune ups, women are saving money by **doing it themselves.**

And while "Do It Yourself" has long been attached to physical home improvement activities, the Recession has pushed DIY into other arenas previously left to experts. Allen Newberry, a high-end hair stylist in Atlanta, says:

> "I still have most of my pre-Recession customers. But now, a certain number of my customers schedule their cuts and colors in longer intervals—waiting in some cases much longer than they should. And a small percentage of them are doing their own color touch ups in between. These are women who never dreamt of doing this before."

As Nice 'n Easy sales have increased, personal service salons in general have suffered.[9] The biweekly mani-pedi and the six-week-cut and color have slowed down as women want to maintain that quality relationship, but can't afford it with the same regularity.

less is . . . green?

Consumers are turning to easy-to-launder apparel and investing in washing machines and dryers with extra bells and whistles that reduce trips to the dry cleaner. The idea of sharing—your home, your tools, and your car—sprung up in formal and informal ways. AirBnB.com helps consumers lower travel costs and enhance vacations by renting stays in homes instead of hotels; it also helps home owners wring more value out of their homes, vacation properties, or apartments. Mass transit use has increased; three-car families with two drivers shed the extra auto, and the use of Zipcar and other ride-sharing services increased. Does everyone in the neighborhood really need a mower and leaf blower or could we share and save money?

The Green and Sustainability movements were underway before the recession, and have mainstreamed during the last four years, in part because of the recession. While a proliferation of new products have appeared with titles of Organic, Green, and Sustainable, many women told us that their commitment to and investment in green isn't completely about the environmental impact. They've gone green in ways that mimic the teachings of their grandparents from the Depression. Reuse, multiuse, repurpose, reduce waste, and, in turn, save money. Water barrels are purchased to catch rainwater and lower outside watering bills; deck and patio containers full of herbs and lettuce appear along with the flowers. There is a commitment to less food waste and, of course, lower gasoline consumption. More carpooling and public transportation use can have a significant impact on the family budget with the halo effect of good community citizenship. It is worth noting, also, that many of these activities bypass the need for dependence on utilities, automobiles, transportation entities, and government regulators. It gives the individual woman a feeling that she may not have to count on others that have proven themselves less than responsible in the past.

less is more

Smart brands will give a woman permission to course correct in response to financially motivated life changes and do so in a way that makes her feel and look smart and savvy. They will give her the feeling of power in the product or the deal. And they will honor the silver linings that the new normal provides. Give her permission to trade down and make it easy.

> Give her permission to trade down **and make it easy.**

But take note: There is a difference between the way younger women and older women approach trading down. Life stage and experience alters how women perceive the value of relationships and things. The universal among women, regardless of cultural background, age, stage, or socioeconomic strata, is that an item or relationship has to deliver real and authentic value. The difference, however, lies in how each of these groups defines value.

Younger women:
an item or relationship
has to deliver
real and authentic
value

A group of recent college graduates gathered in a friend's apartment and told us that they will not buy poor quality for things they love. They want brand names for the things that they love, but for things that "don't matter," the dollar store is just fine. As these young women begin establishing themselves as responsible adults, they say every small purchase counts. "There are certain things that are never going to be a deal. I can't save on gas or rent, so I have to save somewhere else," said 23-year-old Brittany Knight of Atlanta.

chapter 6

Sway

There is in every true woman's heart, a spark of heavenly fire, which lies dormant in the broad daylight of prosperity, but which kindles up and beams and blazes in the dark hour of adversity.

—Washington Irving, *The Sketch Book*

Media headlines hailed 2012 as the year of the woman. In America's 113th Congress, 20 women serve in the Senate and 81 in the House, the most in our country's history. Female Olympians representing the United States, including a pint-sized "Flying Squirrel," graced the American medal stands, bringing home more metal from the London Summer Olympic Games than their male counterparts. And in Silicon Valley, new mom Marissa Mayer was appointed CEO of Yahoo!

While the women of 2012 deserve attention for their significant achievements, we see the years leading out of the dark tunnel of the Great Recession defining an even more notable era of women, one in which everyday females build, maintain, and exhibit influence in their homes, in their workplaces, in their communities, and on a global platform. The authors of this book are women, and can't pass up an opportunity to give an *"atta girl!"* to the sisterhood. But what we are seeing is evidence that women are wielding an even greater measure of influence, an increased level of sway that has been molded and strengthened from the lessons they derived individually and as part of an enormous cohort, from living through and surviving the Recession. While the Great Recession has generated heightened stress for women, it has also delivered personal power to women, as individuals, and as groups and networks. The disastrous economy provided a heightened sensibility about the world, and an even more heightened level of savviness and knowledge about the commercial marketplace. We already see women effectively using what they've learned about getting a better deal from retailers and brands, about putting companies on notice because women everywhere are reading up on them, and expecting transparency in understanding their values and vision. A super majority percentage of the women we surveyed (87 percent) report that they are smarter about the purchases they make since the Recession began in 2007.

> The Great Recession has generated heightened **stress** for women *and* an even greater measure of **influence.**
>
> "I am smarter about the purchases I make":
> **87 percent**

the dynamic of influencers

Marketers and business operators will feel the effects of women having found their voice in the post-Recession marketplace. If in doubt, ask Susan G. Komen for the Cure. Following the decision to eliminate $680,000 in grants to Planned Parenthood for breast cancer screenings and education programs (disclosed in January 2012), the largest nonprofit in the United States devoted to preventing, treating, and curing breast cancer ran into a stone wall of women who criticized the organization for its decision. Using a full arsenal of real-life social networks, social media, local boycott events, and media relations, women ultimately voted with their wallets against the brand and the organization. Within 24 hours of the announcement, donors reacting to the Susan G. Komen Foundation's decision to cut off funding contributed $650,000 directly to Planned Parenthood in a 24-hour period.[1]

"I do my homework. I get all the information I can to make a smart decision, about a product and the company behind it," says Bethany Clark, age 51, from Chicago. "I think in the past I was either too busy to ask the hard questions, or I didn't think about asking them. Now, there is a lot more at stake with the choices I make around purchases or an organization that's getting my time or money."

So who are the women most likely to be tagged an influencer? In 1978, the poster child for an influencer was Lois Gibbs, then a young mother and resident of Love Canal in upstate New York. Gibbs led her neighbors into action to relocate more than 800 households

> No longer a solitary figure on a mission, today's female influencers can create a movement, shut one down, or inspire thousands through **technology.**

impacted by the hazardous materials that had been dumped into Love Canal. Today female activists play an important role in advocating for change; however, unlike Lois Gibbs who was a solitary figure in her mission, we see an important change in the dynamic of influencers and how they work. From the days of Gibbs, Marion Wright Edelman, and even lesser-known advocates, today's female influencers can create a movement, shut one down, or inspire thousands through technology. Already inclined to work as a community instead of as sole practitioners, women with a mission can recommend, inspire, or critique faster, louder, and with greater impact than ever before.

who are these women?

Several years ago, The Haystack Group team audited the profiles of women in our research database in an attempt to construct rudimentary DNA of a typical influencer. We unearthed some universal aspects of American women we found to be the most likely to advocate for or against a cause, or to actively support someone's efforts to make a change. The key markers of an influencer, based on our analysis, paint broad brush strokes of a woman who is eager to learn about the people and companies with whom she does business. She finds satisfaction in gathering information and knowledge and appropriately relishes the power that comes with having facts. She is networked, both in real life and online, providing her a platform to engage others and marshal resources toward a united goal. She is intelligent and tireless, committed and compelling, and unsympathetic if she senses disingenuousness. Jeffrey Kottler, Ph.D., author of *Doing Good: Passion and Commitment for Helping Others* (Taylor & Francis, Inc., 2000), says that altruism can be reciprocal: Humans act benevolently for conscious or unconscious gain. "Theorists talk about it in terms of cost-benefit analysis, as if it's a rational thing," he said in an interview with *Psychology Today*.[2] "We don't do anything selflessly; we do it because it'll come back to us later—someone will owe us something down the line or it will increase our status in the community."

Key markers of women influencers:

1. Finds satisfaction in gathering information and knowledge

2. Relishes the power that comes with having facts

3. Is networked, both in real life and online

4. Marshals resources toward a united goal

5. Is intelligent, tireless, committed & compelling

6. Is unsympathetic if she senses disingenuousness.

Individuals she once respected are increasingly mired in controversy and personalities are finding celebrity by dramatizing conflict. As a result, her default attitude leans toward the critical, so brands and companies will have to demonstrate greater transparency and authenticity and communicate consistently and regularly through multiple channels to engender confidence and instill respect for your brand. Her reluctance to re-establish faith in the institutions she once relied on—financial institutions, schools, houses of worship, community leaders, and non-profits—means she is reframing conversations and messages that suit her needs, and she's spreading her gospel to those in her circles.

sway distribution

One of the most vivid examples that show how women are redistributing their sway is in their willingness to share the most critical information that just years ago they would have kept close to the vest. Like withholding a special ingredient in a sought-after recipe, women previously kept the most valuable information to themselves, rarely sharing the name of their best babysitter or handyman for fear they'd be hired out and unavailable. That "for my information only" mentality has shifted to

REFERRAL NATION
from "for my
information only" to
"mass collaboration"

a "mass collaboration" mentality, paving the way for a broad system of referrals and information-sharing. Motivated by a desire to level the playing field between brands and consumers, women help women win at the game, working to get the best price, the best service, the best options, and the biggest upgrades.

Rather than holding information solely for themselves, women are finding a new kind of influence in sharing a recommendation. With an uptick in families transferred for work and those moving for personal reasons, women are dusting off the wheels of the welcome wagon and supporting the newcomer in their community with information and recommendations for everything from plumbers and pediatricians to restaurants and renovators.

There's power in having the who's who list and in being able to use it. Angie Hicks understood the influence of a referral network when she founded the precursor to Angie's List in 1995. In 2011, Angie's List reached 1.5 million members and went public on NASDAQ (ANGI).[3] From a national organization like Angie's List, to community referral groups like The Milton Sweet Tea Society in Georgia, women appreciate the open exchange of tips and referrals in order to make smart buying decisions and work the most advantageous deals.

The individual power she is harnessing to right her own ship is being combined with the influence of others around her to form a collective in her own community—both physically and virtually. A return to the comfort of a community began in the hours and days after September 11. When faced with the unthinkable, families, neighbors, coworkers, and strangers pulled together for support and solace. The mobilizing behavior borne from a singular event has grown and extended into a movement where women are using their sway to strengthen their own communities. By patronizing neighborhood businesses, affecting change where needed and circling the wagons to leverage safety in numbers, women are using their influence in ways with far more impact than simply making recommendations.

> Sway or influence is about the ability to affect **change**, to be involved in a **process** and to **contribute** to an endeavor.

Marketers should know that for women, sway or influence is more than having the information and shouting it from a rooftop—it's about the ability to affect change, to be involved in a process, and to contribute to an endeavor. From providing valuable input in product development to championing a brand on a retail floor, organizations have taken note of the positive impact an open dialogue with women can foster. In 2004, with an early nod to the swelling co-creation trend and a first in the automotive industry, Volvo unveiled the YCC (Your Concept Car) concept car. With the input of hundreds of female Volvo employees who were involved in nearly all aspects of the design and production of the car, the YCC showcased important features women want in a car. Hans-Olov Olsson, president and chief executive of Volvo, said in an interview with *USA Today* that the company discovered that women want everything in a car that men want in terms of performance and styling, "plus a lot more than male car buyers have ever thought to ask for."[4] Incidentally, women influence about 80 percent of all vehicle purchases every year.[5] While the YCC has never been mass-produced, it is an ideal example of the sway that women can have in a brand's lifecycle from product development through launch and beyond.

make the most of feedback

One of the best strategies to make the most of consumer feedback in the Great Recession era and beyond is to dust off one that is tried and true and underscores the value of an authentic partnership (note we did not go far enough to call this a relationship). Create a platform or channel that allows brands to regularly communicate with female customers, soliciting feedback on products in development through assistance in working out kinks or bugs in another. Follow through, by thanking her for her time and energy, and demonstrate how you're using her input. When the time comes, she's more likely to use her sway—because she's invested in your brand—to influence others and even go so far as to develop content that can be spread throughout the blogosphere or a host of social media platforms. And for the sake of the brand, we'll repeat: follow through and let her know how you're using her input or she might misconstrue your true intentions. Her default position is typically one of distrust; she'll assume you are trying to sway her or worse, tap her opinions without showing that you value her feedback. She'll respect your brand more when you show you value her voice and opinions.

influencing the influencer

So who influences women of influence? According to women we interviewed and those who participated in our online panel, not likely the news media and not necessarily advertisers. Forty-five percent of the women we surveyed say they trust the news media less since the onset of the Great Recession, although that number drops to 38 percent for women in their 30s and to 33 percent of Asian women. More than 60 percent of women (64 percent) say advertisers do not understand their needs today, while 68 percent of Hispanic women and 68 percent of women in their 50s feel advertisers don't get them. Luciana Poliche, age 31, who was born in Argentina, believes that advertisements designed for the Latina overlook the importance of family, which is an important component of the Hispanic culture, as is the importance of showing upward mobility. "In commercials or ads in magazines, I don't see myself reflected as part of an immigrant

NEWS?

Percent of women who say they trust the news media less since the Great Recession began

all women surveyed:
45 percent

women aged 30-39:
38 percent

Asian women:
33 percent

group with a higher standard of living," she says. "I don't buy salsa or tortillas, so those types of ads don't work for me." Jackie Bird of Red Bean Society agrees, "The Latina is still in an acquisition state. The desire to show the success of her journey to families, friends, peers, and her new community is important to her. Brands that fuel the pride women feel in themselves, their journey, and their success will be rewarded."

So where are the loci of influence? A women's touchstone will always be her close community—family and close friends in real life—as well as friends and strangers in online networks. In the television commercial, *State of Disbelief*, advertising agency DDB used a funny approach to underscore a real phenomenon. The advertisement shows a high level of trust that internet users have for their online peer-to-peer networks, sometimes more so than their own real life networks. The commercial was created to showcase State Farm Insurance Company's mobile applications and showed an exchange between a fellow who is using his smart phone to access State Farm's apps after an incident involving his car, and a girl next door who believes everything on the internet. You may scoff, but State Farm isn't that far off the mark. According to information culled from Forrester Research, 32 percent of online consumers trust a stranger's opinion

SAYS WHO?

trust strangers online more than advertisers:

32 percent

trust earned media over any advertising:

92 percent

trust online reviews:

70 percent

on public forums or blogs more than they trust branded advertisements and marketing collateral. Backing this up are statistics from Nielsen's 2012 Global Trust in Advertising report which showed that 92 percent of consumers around the world say they trust earned media, such as recommendations from friends and family, above all other forms of advertising. Online consumer reviews are the second most trusted source of information about brands, with 70 percent of consumers indicating they trust messages on this platform.[6]

Social media sway extends beyond online news sites and social circles. Channels from Facebook to Pinterest provide women the opportunity to live vicariously through others and to inform and be informed. The rise of the Mommy blogger has created an entire cottage industry of product testers and endorsers. Tweeting and critiquing in supersonic time, the bloggers can make or break a product. Pinterest allows women to shop and cook and craft all day through visuals of other people's boards, helping some reconnect with their own personal style or create a new one. What a clever way to give us permission to edit and trade down and show us how.

While CNN and *Time* magazine may not hold sway with women to the degree they have in the past, the information from micro-local news outlets is rising to the top of the influence meter. In a survey conducted for the National Newspaper Association, 71 percent of respondents read a community newspaper at least once a week. Even more telling is the level of engagement between the local news and the reader. More than half of readers (56 percent) had clipped a story or provided a link from the newspaper's website to save or send to someone they know. More than 70 percent believe the accuracy of their local paper is either "good" or "excellent."[7] Community newspapers, neighborhood newsletters and news sites like Patch.com are rising in importance for women who have strong connections to the events taking place in their trading areas, and those who place a high value on learning the food quality scores from the fast food joint down the street.

MICRO NEWS?

read a community paper once/week:

71 percent

save or share articles or links:

56 percent

believes local paper is accurate:

70 percent

chapter 7

Screens

At a dinner table in a casual restaurant, a family sits down to enjoy a meal together. Thirty seconds after being seated, each pulls out his or her mobile phone. This scene is being played out in restaurants, kitchens, dining rooms, in group gatherings and during intimate conversations. In grocery store aisles, at check-out counters, in physician exam rooms, and yes, even bathrooms (why else would one of the top reason phones are replaced is because they're dropped in the toilet?).[1] Aki Iida, head of mobile at Zappos.com relayed a funny story about a customer who placed an order from the lavatory and then tweeted, "Hey, this is the most expensive bathroom trip ever. Thanks, Zappos app."[2]

In our field research for *Hustle*, we observed and, honestly, eavesdropped on mobile phone conversations, peeked over the shoulders of consumers on tablets, watched young women surf on laptops at Starbucks, and discussed television with total strangers. Our key takeaway? America's love affair with the screen, regardless of size, has never been more passionate than it is today.

the trusted friend

While brand loyalty is fleeting and interactions with retailers and service providers are more transaction-oriented, the connection women have with their screens is more like a relationship. The women we interviewed spoke about their mobile devices, televisions, and computers as trusted companions, assigning a level of trust, reliability, and dependability that they don't connect with other products. "My phone doesn't let me down," says Patricia Cain, age 47. "My phone is by my side all the time. I'm connected and informed. How many people can give me that level of knowledge or keep me in the know. None that I know of," she added. According to Pew Internet & American Life Project, 67 percent of cell owners find themselves checking their phone for messages, alerts, or calls—even when they don't notice their phone ringing or vibrating. Forty-four percent of cell owners have slept with their phone next to their bed because they wanted to make sure they didn't miss any calls, text messages, or other updates during the night.[3]

> The women we interviewed spoke about their mobile devices, televisions and computers as **trusted companions**. Their appetite for connectivity is **nearly insatiable**.

Why are screens so important that women have devolved the relationship they had with people, transferring the emotional connection to their devices? Women's circles, or networks, are wide and overlapping. The hats she wears and the roles she has throughout a day bring her in contact with people and organizations beyond just those within her home or business environment. Among the women we interviewed, the appetite for connectivity is nearly insatiable. Television development executive Lee Gaither in *The Guardian* says:

"If you can't stay connected and access mobile content, it makes you feel anxiety. At our core, we're a society that wants what we want when we want it. If we can't access that piece of information or conversation string, we feel we're missing out." "So entrenched are screens in a woman's life that she spends twice as much time a day with her mobile phone, television, and computer than she does with a spouse. And 30 minutes of the time she spends with her spouse is typically devoted to watching television."[4]

The screens in her life help her get the most with her money and the most out of her time. Mobile devices, computers, and television have provided women access to the content she needs, putting power right where she wants it—in her own hands. Screens entertain, they inform, they connect. Screens deliver a palm-sized platform to persuade, to share, and they help women master the deal. Aided by daily deals and experts in consumer affairs, women are making the most of their time and their dollars by preparing for a purchase in advance and price-checking on the spot. Her GPS-enabled smartphone gets her from the office to the little league game via the most efficient route. In the two minutes she sits at a traffic light, she can deposit a check courtesy of a Bank of America app on her iPhone. She can download a meal plan and shopping list for dinner, access weekly sales and coupons and refill a prescription all through the Publix grocery store app. She can check email, purchase movie tickets for a Saturday date night, update her calorie count to stick to her diet, watch a video while sitting in the bleachers and order the cutest chenille throw pillow during a time out. All from her trusted screen.

the screen at retail

Laura Houston is a strategic consumer who shops with a binder of coupons and printed deals cross-referenced by store and item. She knows how to maximize savings to get 10 tubes of toothpaste for free. "I started doing this when the Recession hit. Now I do this for the power," she says. "I know which store takes competitor coupons and which price match. It takes time but it's worth it. When you realize you've saved $80, you win." While the majority of coupon users con-

people in the
US who redeem
digital coupons:

2012: 92.5 million
2014: 100+ million

tinue to redeem promotions found in print publications and circulars, eMarketer, a research company that
creates reports that cover digital marketing, media, and
commerce, estimates that 92.5 million people in the
U.S. redeemed a digital coupon in 2012. By 2014, the
number of U.S. adult digital coupon users will surpass
100 million. By 2014, one in four mobile phone users will redeem a coupon via a mobile device.[5] Daily deal sites like Bradsdeals.com and apps offering time-sensitive deals have attracted a new audience that has never before used mobile coupons.[6]

"content" not "ads"

So how are marketers responding? "The way consumers are using media has shifted dramatically," says Patricia Wilson, founder of Brand Cottage, a media agency providing integrated communica-tions across all media platforms. "Women are using screens to make life easier. Technology is driving everything and brands will follow. No longer are marketers creating ads; they are creating content," Wilson said. "You can no longer just sell to your consumer. You must also solve something for her." This approach has turned traditional advertising on its ear as the big idea often begins with a cool use of a screen and works back to the creative process. The siloed thinking of the past, in which linear marketing planning began with a planner and ended with a production person, won't work anymore. If your agencies and consultants aren't full of alpha creative visionaries in every department, you might want to rethink your structure—or your relationships.

The new darlings of social media, like Instagram, websites, apps, and games can be less costly to implement and can be produced more spontaneously. But they shouldn't overshadow the power of the old screens of television and print—or even that non-screen, radio. More television is being bought today than ever before. At last, your television spot doesn't have to say it "all"—it can do its highest and best job to engage emotionally and build awareness. Your consumer can and will get all the other needed information on your website, the reviews on social media, product demos on YouTube, and coupons and advice from Bradsdeals.com. And you can post the spot on any or all of the above to garner even more impressions. While their spots weren't necessarily geared for females, power brands Nike, Pepsi, and Volkswagen were the most watched ads on YouTube in 2012, earning as many organic views as paid views throughout the year.[7] Chipotle Mexican Grill's national TV ad—the first in the restaurant chain's 18-year history—is a full version of a two-minute animated video originally featured on YouTube. Clearly, an inspired television spot that is worth sharing is more valuable than ever before.

The community manager, the content manager, the user experience manager are now the engineers of the successful brand. They help integrate and curate these multiple platforms for the highest degree of success. Critical jobs today, they barely existed prior to the Recession. While the old days of product placement advertising in programming has roared back into the mainstream, marketing departments, agencies, and consultants must become more collaborative, not just internally, but also externally. Remain vigilant for partnerships with other brands, media, programming, and even non-profit organizations.

Think differently about the team composition and leadership. Assign your best facilitators and motivators to lead these collaborations, not necessarily your best strategist. Fill the team with specialized experts who can think in and out of their own boxes.

the powerful media women of 2012

As we were deep in the editing of *Hustle*, *Forbes* published its list of Most Powerful Women of 2012.[8] What we found striking about the women on the 2012 list was how many represent the multi-faceted media industry and how many are setting the agenda and driving the content delivered to screens we devour on a daily basis. Jill Abramson, executive editor of *The New York Times*, is leading a 161-year-old print publication into the digital age. Arianna Huffington grew the online newspaper she founded into a leading news source and winner of a Pulitzer Prize. Anne Sweeney, co-chairman of Disney Media Networks and president of Disney/ABC Television Group, oversees 100 channels that reach 600 million viewers. Amy Pascal, co-chairman, Sony Pictures Entertainment, is behind some of the biggest cinematic blockbusters today, and in her role at Sony Pictures Television; the network is now in 754 million homes. Sue Naegle, president of HBO Entertainment, oversees all series programming and specials. Under her leadership, HBO was nominated for 81 Prime Time Emmy Awards in 2012—the most of any television network. Ellen DeGeneres, star and executive producer of *The Ellen Show*, makes news and reports on it. The influence of Sue Gardner, executive director of the non-profit Wikimedia Foundation, is felt every time we research a topic on Wikipedia.

Over the course of six decades, when consumers went from purely a viewing public whose only choice in content was whether to watch

Howdy Doody or *Captain Video*, to creative connoisseurs of media—inspiring content, creating it, and using it women are on both sides of the screen. They are producing and creating the messages and images across the screen portfolio that consumers read, follow, play, access, view, download, and digest.

Thanks to the Great Recession, women have an across-the-board distrust of many institutions they once held in high esteem. Frustrated and ready to speak, they put down their pencils and picked up their laptops; they have something to say. According to the Pew Research Center's Internet & American Life Project, approximately 14 percent of women who are online in the United States write blogs.[9] Clearly, they have something to say. Ask Heather B. Armstrong, one of the most successful bloggers in the country, who is the creative force behind Dooce.com. What started as a series of humorous rants and posts in 2001 turned into a media darling and extensions into other platforms, including several books, most recently *It Sucked and Then I Cried* (Simon Spotlight Entertainment, 2009). An average of 300,000 people follow the blog daily, even more for moments in time

> An inspired television spot that is worth sharing is more valuable than ever before—let YouTube, Facebook and Twitter **extend that initial investment.**

like the birth of Armstrong's second child, and Armstrong boasts more than 850,000 Twitter followers.[10] Ree Drummond, *aka* The Pioneer Woman, may be the best-known of today's women bloggers. The Pioneer Woman has turned what began as a "blog thing" into a cottage industry replete with cookbooks, children's books, television programs, and a movie starring Reese Witherspoon.[11]

Television development executive Lee Gaither believes the absorption of media into daily life isn't considered a luxury because it's happened so incrementally. "There was a natural progression from the rotary dial to the touchtone dial to the portable to analog mobile phones to digital—we didn't comprehend the extraordinary changes in how we were building or living our lives," said Gaither. "We quickly went from living in a defined community and consuming information and entertainment chosen for us, to having access to the world at large and driving the content being developed and delivered on a universal stage." Soon, if what we are seeing as the worlds of technology—hardware, software, and content—intersect, we'll see one screen that can do everything, packaged and sold in pocket-size and biggie-sized depending on the consumer's appetite.

chapter 8

Sages

W hen my husband and I toyed with the idea of selling our home, we were certain we were facing significant costs to update it—expand a room here, add closets there—and before making a move sought the advice from a trusted friend and realtor. She gave us sage advice: don't worry about adding on or building out. Just make what you have pristine. Women across the country are living these words of wisdom as they rebuild their financial, physical, and emotional lives from the Great Recession. No longer burdened with the goal of acquiring or expanding, woman are learning and reinforcing ways to innovate, improve, and renovate what they already have. This is reflected as well in a return to the basics, a consumer shift that Maid Brigade recognized in its customer base. The firm is one of the country's leading franchise home-cleaning services and the first to offer and market an integrated in-home Green cleaning service.

> Women are learning and reinforcing ways to **innovate, improve and renovate** what she already has. She is looking for brands that help her **edit, maintain, upgrade or repurpose.**

"Before the economy turned down, women had time and space to think about the impact of a green cleaning approach and the health of their home," said Cloud Q. Conrad, Vice President of Brand Strategies for Maid Brigade. "We focused our messaging on the certified green clean platform, and had excellent traction. When the economic downturn settled in, our customer base as a whole was forced to make discriminating choices, between a clean house and a green, healthy home. The value of the experience transformed almost overnight. So we had to re-adapt and that meant moving away from our differentiated message to one that communicated we understand her needs are more basic right now. Our customers really want to take care of their homes and enjoy living in them. That's what we're here to do."

We see this in the way she is looking for brands that help her edit, maintain, upgrade or repurpose the things she owns. She, with the aid of brand partners, is finding new uses for the things she has, streamlining how she lives her life, improving the value or extending the utility of products already in her home, and customizing possessions to suit her new normal.

girls just want to have fun

According to psychologists, there is a real trauma that is experienced when people go through prolonged periods of stress or crisis. Financial woes are one of the most common trauma-inducing triggers. Sales of anti-depressants have skyrocketed as have increases in the number of admissions to substance abuse rehabilitation centers.[1] The good news, though, is that many mental health counselors are finding a strong thread of resiliency in the clients they counsel. "Women are so resilient and creative in the ways they find to make their multidimensional lives work," said psychotherapist Nancy Maseng, with a practice in South Carolina that caters specifically to the needs of women. "For the most part I see women who adapt and deal, and a little emotional support goes a long way."

To fortify their bank accounts and their psyches, women have tweaked their outlooks to ones of cautious optimism in ways that give them relief from the sometimes repressive frugality of life without sacrificing the stability they've regained. One of the interesting conversations we had was with a group of women from the Northeast who talked about the way they subconsciously choreograph the balance between their hangover from stress and anxiety and a real desire for fun. By day, Ellen Barnard is an executive producer for a media production company. By night, she is a member of a neighborhood knitting group. "I get to do something I really enjoy and do it with other people who like to do the same thing," she says. "The world is a much more stressful place now. We have so much information coming at us all the time. News and stories are constant and we have to keep up with them. The knitting group helps slow everything down. If I never finished something I wouldn't really care; it's just really about being in this community of people you like. The knitting is what brought us together and an activity we share with no pressure or end goal." Whether the outlet is a book club, craft group, or structured card games like Bunko, Mahjong, or Bridge, women crave the opportunity to be together. And the commitment to these times with girlfriends is becoming more and more important. The cost of entry is low, and in this totally connected world of technology, women tell us that they need personal interaction now more than ever before. Female friendships are stress busters. The "Girls Night Out" has even evolved to a cheeky set of hostess gifts and bar brands like WINO's (Women in Need of Sanity). Marketers who give them permission

> The commitment to **girlfriend time** is becoming more important. Female friendships are stress busters.

and even an outlet to let go of their stress and worry and rediscover themselves, will be rewarded.

As their financial condition improves and chaos is supplanted by stability, women are becoming more receptive to seeing the humor in life and yes, even joy. As a result, they are more willing to allow for small pleasures that were verboten even a year ago, from basics like socks, to cupcakes and perfume. For an article in *The New York Times*, Vicki G. Morwitz, a professor of marketing at the Stern School of Business at New York University offered, "When the crisis hit and people really started to feel a pinch in their pocketbooks, they started to spend less across the board, especially in discretionary kinds of things." She added, "But it's difficult, I think, for people to do that for a long time, even when they need to."[2]

In her effort to rebuild on footing that is becoming more stable, she is more willing to give a new service or product a try, particularly if it is a business based in her personal trading area and is backed by a personal recommendation, but she is wary of committing. In a service category that could easily be confused as a luxury offering, Scottsdale-based Massage Envy has seen growth even during the economic downturn. Marcy Bartlett, manager of one of the most successful units in the Southeast described the secret to her unit's success, "We understand that there are nuances in how we present our service to consumers—women especially. At first, they are opposed to the idea of a contract. They don't want to commit. Our clientele is very thorough; they really think things through and have to take time to consider the commitment aspect of our services. So we don't

> In her effort to rebuild on footing that is becoming more stable, she is more willing to give a new service or product a try but is wary of committing in the post-Recession world.

make them; we let it be their choice. We give them a much-needed service that they assume costs much more than the bill we present at the end of the massage. We talk about our services as therapeutic, an approach to wellness, and an important component to their health. We even provide receipts so they can file for flex spending. Ultimately they end up bonding with their therapist and it's no longer a commitment to Massage Envy but it evolves into a commitment they make to their own health. If you get to that stage, you know you have a good relationship with your customer."

building guarded appreciation

For the foreseeable future, blind loyalty will be all but extinct. It will be replaced by guarded appreciation for companies and brands that demonstrate mutual respect, giving women valuable tools, resources, information, and knowledge. Today's typical woman is using products and brands wisely. She has done her homework on generics and private labels and will know when the store label ups the ante by offering super-soft toilet paper manufactured with the same advanced technology as the national brands.

Far from a store brand, Seventh Generation is the nation's leading brand of household and personal care products that help protect human health and the environment. In 2012, Seventh Generation teamed with *Real Simple* magazine to launch the Cleanhouse Challenge, an interactive game where users explore a virtual house and discover coupons and prizes, while learning about how to keep a greener, healthier home. The Challenge was hosted at RealSimple.com, SeventhGeneration.com and the Seventh Generation Facebook page. Consumers who visited each room in the online home took away tips, advice, and statistics made available through pop-up videos. After touring each room, visitors were rewarded with coupons for discounts on Seventh Generation products and Facebook badges to show their expertise in keeping a green home. Seventh Generation donated $10 (maximum of $15,000) to environmental non-profit 350.org for every user who completed every room of the house. Seventh Generation demonstrated respect for consumers with an interest in green cleaning by providing useful information using a fun and entertaining platform, making women feel good about themselves and about choosing Seventh Generation products.

Whether you are a cola aficionado or prefer only an occasional fizzy drink, Sodastream may be one of the most interesting new products available to consumers. This home carbonation system speaks to women because it eliminates plastic bottles, reducing landfill waste and the carbon footprint, and offers 100 flavors in full-sugar and diet varieties. Plus, there is a range of product types so you can customize your machine. Guys may like this for the gadgetry involved, but women we've interviewed appreciate the multi-functional, solution-oriented, and environmental aspects of a "really cool" appliance.

Yogurt has come a long way from limited varieties of fruit on the bottom or blended cups. Today consumers can choose from an endless array of artisanal options, exotic flavors, and styles ranging from Greek, New Zealand, and even Icelandic, produced by companies as ubiquitous as Chobani or family-operated like Dreaming Cow. The yogurt category has experienced tremendous growth and according to NPD Group, nearly one in three individuals eats yogurt regularly.[3] Thanks to great taste, clever marketing and product innovation, yogurt manufacturers are giving consumers an enjoyable, healthy product at an affordable price point. Backed by attributes of gastric-friendly bacteria and higher protein content, this pocket-size product drives huge revenues. And consumers are rewarding the category by taking the versatility of the food and running with it, sometimes literally. "I'll spend $1.25 for a cup of yogurt," said Genevieve Bouts. "They've given me a great alternative for a meal replacement and suggestions for how to use yogurt as a bakery recipe ingredient so I pinned them to my Pinterest light-foods board." New Yorker and Millennial Genevieve Bouts added, "I'm going Mach 10 during the day and that little container is a great pick me up snack. Sometimes it is breakfast and lunch."

refocus on the consumer

Companies and brands that have successfully weathered the economic storm have learned a lot of lessons. Their schooling has been far more than how to cut costs to squeeze out greater margin, but also to refocus on their most productive asset—their consumer. Some of the most valuable learning has come from those who placed their consumer front and center and built best practices around how to most efficiently and effectively deliver what she wants and make it easy for her to include the brand in her consideration set. There are stories of triumph in every consumer category—brands that remained transparent and true to their mission, unwavering in communicating that charge. The stories of failure are often from companies and brands that over-promised and under-delivered, losing their way because they failed to keep customers at the core of their business, marketing, and communications strategies.

The companies that have managed to successfully adapt to the post-Recession woman have done so through a series of steps and measures—by taking an unvarnished audit of their strengths and their weaknesses; by making a difference in her community; by entertaining her when she needed it most; and by making it easier for her to be a woman wearing a wide assortment of hats in very trying times. This falls in the category of products that don't let her down and are backed by a guarantee. Among the most straightforward feats is to do what you say you're going to do, or ensure that your product does what you say it will do.

"I love to vacuum," said stay-at-home mom Robin Feldman. "It's something you have to do, and you can see the result immediately. But it's an awful chore if your vacuum cleaner doesn't work." This sentiment shared by women, especially those with children and pets in the home, makes products like Dyson vacuum cleaners particularly noteworthy. The inventor and founder, James Dyson, who is featured in the company's advertising, spent 15 years designing and making 5,127 prototypes before he launched the DC01 vacuum cleaner. The company's commitment to producing a product that works is fundamental to the rave reviews the products receive from consumers online and in real life. Vera Casdia posted the following on Amazon. com in December 2008: "The vacuum of my dreams! I have never reviewed a product before, but this vacuum cleaner has me so excited that I had to share it with someone. I really love this machine!"

the "slasher" workforce

Women have always been multi-taskers at home and are now leveraging that mentality and ability to adapt their previous "regular" jobs into the new "slasher" workforce. Today's women are recreating the workplace by customizing and personalizing job types and work styles to suit their needs and situation. What might have been previously thought of as a consultant or freelancer, "slashers" are cobbling together a string of jobs and work titles. "I'm a writer/marketer/special events planner," said one former advertising agency executive. While being a "slasher" provides benefits ranging from a flexible work schedule and work location, "slashing" also requires that women have even more balls in the air—often with less income and fewer benefits. Free time remains elusive, even for the "slasher." Marketers need to give her products, services, customer service, sales support, and technology that deliver time instead of depriving her of this valuable commodity.

> Today's women are recreating the workplace by **customizing and personalizing** job types and work styles to suit their needs and situation.

Since the final months of 2008, women have evolved into hybrid consumers who are taking stock in some of the lessons learned and re-entering the marketplace with a new persona and a new intent. Women appreciate understanding why you believe in your product and how it is going to make a difference in their lives. Show them in demonstrable terms why the price is right. Invite them in for a look behind the brand and then make it worth their while to bring it in to their homes.

It's more important than ever to stay in touch with your consumer and ask her how she likes her experience with your product, service, or brand. It's equally important to reward her for taking time to provide the feedback.

chapter 9

Seers

"You've got to think about big things while you're doing small
things, so that all the small things go in the right direction."

—Alvin Toffler

M arketing to women who have endured the Great Recession
and are marked by its impact is like juggling fire: the
smallest miscalculation and somebody gets burned.
Navigating the marketplace in the post-Recession era requires
discipline, focus, and a steady hand, along with an understanding of
how women will behave and why. Here are a few of the questions
that deserve serious attention:

- How does one establish or rebuild a bond with a
  consumer who is primarily interested in a superior
  transaction rather than a relationship?
- How does one underscore the unique selling proposition
  of an established brand when she is focused on the deal?
- How do you set forth a pricing strategy in a Hustle
  economy?

- When she is a power user of technology, how do you ensure your brand is present before, during, and after every transaction?

- How do you navigate the retail landscape that is quickly evolving?

And, by the way, it's never been harder to manage an integrated communications and marketing program of paid, earned, and owned strategies.

Thanks to the trauma they experienced from the disastrous economy, women are subconsciously waiting for the other Jimmy Choo to fall from the sky, hopefully with a steep discount attached. Mild concern escalates to fear when headlines scream "Major Crash Ahead for U.S. Investors," and "Why Inflation is Imminent."[1] The talk-news circuit eats up alarming predictions from media-friendly investors who hit the airwaves plugging books and speeches and inflaming the fears of vulnerable viewers. With a dynamic economic backdrop, how do you map out a strategy for your brand or company when your target consumer is less trusting, slower to purchase, hyper-vigilant, hyper-educated, fixated on a discount and using all the screens available to determine if you should be part of her consideration set? We see six scenarios playing out as consumers adapt to a post-Recession life.

Six Lessons Every Marketer Should Learn in a Post-Recession World

1. How to make shopping mean more than a discount.

2. How to prepare for the deal marketplace to shift.

3. How to cure her Frugality Fatigue.

4. How to make the most of mobile.

5. How to be relevant to women.

6. How to earn her respect.

1. Showrooming v. Showrooms

(Or, How to make shopping mean more than a discount.)

Whether your responsibility is to move a brand off the drawing board and onto the retail floor or to drive traffic to a local business, or even create the next must-have mobile app, you need to be well-versed in two key factors that are rapidly changing the retail landscape. First, as we have described throughout this book, women are using multiple technologies in ways that are dramatically changing their behavior on the retail floor. Second, they are addicted to the discount.

JC Penney

These consumer behaviors are working at cross-purposes for department store JC Penney. In an effort to overhaul and update its brand, JC Penney, under the leadership of CEO Ron Johnson who developed Apple, Inc.'s chain of eponymous stores, announced that it would roll out redesigned stores where boutiques within the store would feature the wares of interesting designers. The intended outcome of this move was to help women access fresh, high-quality merchandise at everyday fair prices without needing to rely on sales, discounts, and coupons. What JC Penney didn't count on was the ingrained coupon-clipping behavior of its loyal female shoppers. Now, the century-old retailer has alienated its established customer base and been slow to draw in Millennials, who are vital to the strategy. In announcing earnings for the fourth quarter of 2012, JC Penney reported sales were down nearly 30 percent from the previous year[2] and merchandise vendors are unhappy. The company has brought back sales and coupons, JC Penney calls them "gifts," for its loyal shoppers. In a story for NPR's *Morning Edition/Planet Money* segment, retail analyst Rafi Mohammed described CEO Johnson's approach as, "He sort of said sales were akin to drugs, and he was trying to wean customers off drugs." Adding, "It didn't work. The old customers really did love clipping coupons and waiting for sales."[3]

We like what JC Penney is trying to do. A marketplace can't survive if the only proposition is a deep discount, so a strategy to encourage consumers to move past a discount mindset is prudent. Hard to accomplish, but smart. The challenge is this: How do you replace the financial benefit and emotional rush that a woman gets from executing on a fabulous deal. You'll have to replace it with something as fulfilling and valuable. This is where technology, consumer-empowering information, and satisfaction come in to play. A trip to the store isn't just about the purchase anymore. It's a field trip, like going to the Smithsonian, where a visitor can interact with the exhibits for a more meaningful, personal experience.

Webvan

First, a trip back in time. We miss Webvan. Anyone who didn't experience the joys of ordering groceries online and having them delivered to your kitchen counter in 2001, really missed out on something special. The problem was not Webvan's service. Customers, especially mothers, appreciated the service, rewarding it with an 89 percent satisfaction rating on Epinions.com.[4] The fatal flaws were that online grocery shopping was a decade before its time; Webvan aggressively expanded to a wide network of markets, and it ran out of operating cash before the general market could catch up to the concept.

What would happen if Webvan was reintroduced today: If it were backed by brand assets important to women, like convenience, Green, and locally sourced? And, in a time when 22 percent of women make an online purchase every day?[5] A time when a survey from Robert Half Technology notes that 60 percent of employers have to block online shopping from company computers?[6] While not a brick and mortar store, it could have been. The online ordering aspect could have easily been an extension to a physical location. The real story here is that Webvan offered a great proposition: fair pricing, great customer service, easy to use, an easy-to-understand benefit (time savings), and a smart use of technology.

the American pastime

In 2003, James Farrell, a professor of history and American studies at St. Olaf College, claimed that shopping was America's favorite pastime.[7] While Farrell's book, *One Nation Under Goods: Malls and the Seductions of American Shopping* (Smithsonian, 2003), talks most about the mall shopper experience, today's pastime continues not just in brick and mortar malls, but pop-up shops, online sites, flash deals, and consumer-run swap-and-sell sites like Freecycle and Share. Retailers must consider carefully what they want their "retail" presence to be. Is your brand appropriate and nimble enough to fit multiple formats? Or, is your brand dependent on certain characteristics of "place?" Regardless, your place of sale needs to give your target customer opportunities to be part of the experience and to make her feel smart and somewhat in control. Make it interesting, entertaining and rewarding, not time intensive. And offer meaningful, connective, fresh content to keep her coming back.

As a retailer and a brand, how do you reconfigure the shopping and purchasing experience to embrace the reality of how women buy today? How do you inspire a transaction between consumer and your brand when the gatekeeper is in the midst of dynamic shifts?

We suggest looking at the mash up of the best aspects of retail and online shopping, where you deliver a boutique experience online or a compelling technology at the point of sale in a traditional retail environment. Imagine the possibilities if a shopping cart had a dashboard outfitted with GPS to help a consumer navigate the sales floor, with mobile price-checking capabilities making the bulky wand a relic. The dashboard might also allow product reviews from some of the best reference sites, point her to special insider deals within the brick and mortar environment, and use the latest collaborative filtering software to customize options just for her. What if the contents of the cart were tallied and an estimated total sale price displayed prior to reaching the check-out line? What if all this were available in a phantom version in an online storefront?

2. What's The Big Deal?

Prepare for the deal marketplace to shift. Groupon and other deal sites are struggling to keep a good inventory of customized product for today's mega-deal shopper and working to deliver deals that are unique and differentiated. "Big daddy" Groupon is feeling the pressure, and a shift in the C-suite signals even more changes to come. If your brand strategy includes a discount, then make sure your deal is meaningful or unique. Make the offer an event—something special that she can't access all the time. And don't elevate deal-making as the centerpiece of your strategy unless cutting prices is your vision of the future.

More than half of consumers (52 percent) said they felt overwhelmed by the number of daily deals they receive.[8] From this dissatisfaction, services like Unsubscribe from Google are providing apps that will crawl through your emails to safely remove you from daily deals and other social applications, eliminating the early chorus of pings on your iPhone as they all roll in. "When I got an offer for a discounted bouncy jump birthday castle for little kids, I unsubscribed," said a mother of two college students. "Clearly they were scraping bottom to send me a deal, any deal. I don't need that clogging up my inbox. What used to be a really great service became junk mail."

3. Curing Frugality Fatigue

With frugality fatigue as a headwind, consumers have become weary of a life of austerity and ready to consider select purchases in a range of categories. Women will begin to replace basics, from personal items to services and products for the home, that they did without at the height of Recession. As a brand or service offering, you can help them evolve from extreme streamlining into a more balanced approach to spending. Demonstrate how your product will help her recalibrate the introduction of additional brands into her home and take on new activities or those that have been in a holding pattern. She will consider products that meet her evolved criteria set:

- Does it make me feel smart? Did I learn something?
- Did I enjoy the experience?
- Do they get me?
- Did I get a good value? Or better yet, a great one?
- Does it fit into my edited life—multipurpose, easy to maintain and store, versatile?
- Was my user experience convenient and easy to navigate?
- Does it make me feel like I'm no longer on an austerity plan? (This is a big one!)
- Does it require a long-term commitment?

There is a staggering amount of pent up demand among the

women that we spoke with. They are tired of saying no to their kids, tired of dreading gifting occasions, and tired of their out-of-date wardrobes. Your challenge in reaching this shopper will be to find a way to invite her out for a special occasion and give her permission to have some fun with your product or service. Life does not have to be so serious.

4. Swipe It

Soon the use of the digital wallet will become *de rigueur* and even the smallest of craft show artists will be accepting credit card payments through a $10 attachment to their smartphones. The morphing and melding of mobile technologies to be a one-stop portal for all things associated with revenue means that your brand must communicate its premise in a big way, on a small screen, with fewer and fewer characters. Content in these formats requires a return to the need for an economy of word usage and quality, and compelling video images that were once exclusive to television.

> Your brand must communicate its premise in a big way, on a small screen, with fewer and fewer characters.

Don't assume that technology is just for the young. Boomer women are the fastest adapters of new technology and social media, and the Great Recession only fueled their passion. A trip to the Apple store on any given day means a wait in line as the crowds of Baby Boomer women get personal coaching from their "Genius" to manage a growing set of technology devices. These are the women with potentially the greatest spending power and most time to shop. Never assume that the tablet is a toy for the young—for women, young and old, it's a power tool.

5. Go With The Flo

This statistic is worth repeating: Sixty-four percent of the women we surveyed say that advertisers do not understand their needs today. At a time when your brand needs to become or remain part of her consideration set and prove to be a worthwhile transaction, she thinks you don't get her. So move over Betty Crocker, it's time to go with the Flo.

The Progressive Insurance lady is one of the best examples of how a brand speaks to women with a message that's meaningful and through an icon that makes it a joy to buy insurance. Flo is helpful and pleasant, appropriately sassy, and comforting, at a time when those attributes are hard to come by in everyday real-world interactions. The popularity of Flo can be found on Twitter, YouTube, and Facebook, where there are more than a handful of separate sites created for Flo. Her iconic presence has extended beyond the television screen to social, mobile, games, print, radio, and even into the world of Halloween costumes. A wig, a name tag, and a white apron and you're good to go.

What makes Flo work for the Progressive brand is the understated, yet powerful, respect it shows women and the emphasis on helping a woman solve a problem with an easy solution. Simplify the concept. In a Recessionary world, there's no room for anything overly complicated, so don't overcomplicate it. Finally, remain true to your brand. The post-Recession consumer is more authentic than ever, and she expects the same from brands. Peter Hempel, CEO and president of DDB New York, offered the following advice for advertisers and marketers:

> "Continue to treat women like real people, reflect their authenticity. Demonstrate honesty in your approach. We stand behind

the credo that there is nothing more impactful than understanding the true nature of women."

One-of-a-kind Flo offers up insurance in easy to understand boxes, sweetly scoffs at those who make it complicated, and even price shops for you. No wonder everyone but the competition loves Flo.

6. Make Her Day

A popular customer-service and sales-training gimmick in the early days of the millennium was the FISH! Philosophy. It was explained in a small book about how the whacky fish-throwing antics of the Pike Place Fish Market were the epitome of the perfect customer experience. A key highlight was something called "Make Her Day." Give her some thing, some experience, some deal, or some story that she isn't expecting, and she will talk about it.

We believe that "Making Her Day" can help move her out of the comfort zone of suspicion and begin to rid her of some of the pent-up distrust creep. As a result, she'll be open to trying new things and reacquaint herself with her wallet. The idea has been somewhat mainstreamed through the "Pay It Forward" movement.

Janet Simmons, one of our panelists, told a story about a perception-shifting experience at a neighborhood fast-food drive-up window during the lunch hour rush. As she pulled up to the window, prepared to hand the cashier her debit card, he said, "That's not necessary. The driver in front paid for your lunch and asked that I tell you to have a nice day." Stunned, Janet thanked him and proceeded to pay the bill for the patron behind her. The next week, the driver in front of her at a toll booth paid her toll in a rolling-style pay it forward.

What if brands did the same thing? Look for opportunities to deliver a nice surprise to your consumer. She's had enough of the bad surprises. In a nod to our sorely missed defunct online grocer, one of the added benefits of ordering through Webvan was the extra something that they surprised you with every week. It might have been a couple of perfect oranges or a sample of a new product. It was something unexpected that made us smile and like them even more than for their excellent everything else.

chapter 10

2020 in 20/20

It's not easy being green
It seems you blend in with so many other ordinary things
And people tend to pass you over
'Cause you're not standing out
Like flashy sparkles on the water
Or stars in the sky.[1]

Kermit the Frog

T he iconic milepost year 2020 is just around the corner, only seven holiday shopping seasons away. Anyone responsible for a brand, managing a product, or running a business understands the delicate balance between serving your customers today, preparing for tomorrow, and laying the groundwork for the future.

Our research and preparation for the writing of *Hustle* allowed us to talk with more than a thousand women coast-to-coast, all of whom had that second X chromosome, yet represent a wide spectrum of socio-economic, educational, and cultural influences. Our research confirmed our hunch—the Great Recession is having more than a passing effect on women, all women, and that those effects will influence them throughout the years to come. The research also revealed some nuances among multi-cultural women that are vital to creating successful marketing campaigns and ensuring a healthy brand or business in 2020.

By 2020, the population in the United States will look different and marketers can't afford to be color-blind. The new population will reflect a rise in the number of Latinos who will call the United States home. African-American consumers, representing nearly 14 percent of the U.S. population, are still the largest racial minority group in America.[2] This dynamic, vital, and growing segment will have a projected buying power of more than $1.1 trillion and "remain at the forefront of social trends and media consumption."[3]

DYNAMIC?
The American workplace in 2020
white:
63 percent
Latino:
30 percent
women:
50 percent

By 2020, the American workplace will be more diverse: 63 percent white, 30 percent Latino, and 50 percent female. Four or even five generations, from Boomers to Generation 2020, will be working at once.[4]

America's melting pot of women share similar traits even as they reflect diverse experiences, cultures, and traditions. The importance of inter-generational relationships and families crosses all groups. Many of the women responsible for a lion's share of purchases are younger than Caucasian women. They enjoy the experience of shopping, and for many, brick-and-mortar shopping is a family outing or a group-oriented social experience. And they are prolific users of mobile technology in the retail setting.

There are excellent resources that can guide and help you understand the multi-cultural women in America, including consultancies such as New York–based Red Bean Society or California-based New

American Dimensions. These experts can help put context around the interesting facts that we unearthed in our research, explaining why Hispanic women seemed to be the least surprised of the groups we surveyed about the severity and the duration of the Great Recession. Or, why Latinas said that the Great Recession affected relationships with family and friends to a greater degree than other cultural groups. Or even, that they reported the greatest drop in brand loyalty and are the group declaring that advertisers do not understand them.

Why would nearly one-third of all African-American women report that the Great Recession had a positive impact on their lives? Half of the women in this multi-cultural group, compared to 64 percent of Asian women, reveal they are less trusting overall as a result of the Great Recession. And hands down, the typical African American is the most innovative when it comes to getting or purchasing the things she needs in a down economy.

As is often the case with research, ours not only proved our hypotheses but opened the door to many questions that couldn't be answered in the pages of *Hustle*. We encourage you to explore the "whats" and "whys" of your vital consumer and put important context around the multi-cultural, age, and even geographic parameters that reflect who she is and why she buys the way she does. Use that knowledge to make the transaction you offer her just a little bit better with the goal that long before 2020, she'll be ready to commit to you.

Acknowledgments

Transforming an idea into 20,000 words is a collaborative effort and impossible without the contributions of many talented and supportive individuals. The authors would like to thank the women who participated in the qualitative and quantitative research studies for this book, who shared their time, their homes and their insights and brought the idea of Hustle to life. These women appear throughout the pages of this book and although their identities are cloaked, their feelings and beliefs are authentic. Many professionals who work in the marketing, media, public relations, and social science fields served as sounding boards and cheerleaders, providing inspiration, advice, and expert commentary. Thank you to the team at Paramount Market Publishing who responded to our proposal in a matter of hours with a resounding "Yes!" It has been a pleasure working with you. A huge thank you to the team at LiveWire Research who found merit in our hypothesis and worked in partnership with us to put quantitative data around a woman's intuition. Erika Snayd and Denise Brooks, you're the best. Renee Cassard, a big shout-out to you for introducing us to LiveWire.

Bonnie would like to acknowledge Frederick Taylor of Tomorrow Pictures, who is a creative life force. It has been a pleasure to call you colleague and friend for twenty-plus years. Thank you for inspiring the title of this book and always reminding me (when I needed to hear it most) that all this is important. To the Chaloux family, thank you for so graciously offering up the peace and solitude of your vacation home; what a great place to try to channel Grisham. Many thanks to the individuals who helped get the book project off the ground, including Kim Gonano, who thought the whole idea was cool, and to dear friend Lynnette McIntire who contributed superb editing to the endeavor and brought dinner when my family thought I'd forgotten how to cook. The project couldn't have gotten a better vote of confidence than your words, "Don't bother me. I want to keep reading." To Dr. Robert Simmermon, co-founder of The Haystack Group, you helped bring a new approach to the fields of marketing and communications and shined a light on the complex intersection between the human psyche and marketing. Colleagues and clients are the better for your pioneering insights. Many thanks to the team at The Haystack Group, who kept the machine running while this book took on a life of its own. To my children—Madison, Jacob, and Wendy—you are the lights of my life. You teach me everyday what it means to love and cherish what is in front of us and live in the moment. You inspire me and cheer me on even when I am doing something that has nothing to do with being your mom. To my parents, Dr. Morgan Worthy and Linda Worthy, you are tough acts to follow. Finally, to my husband, please keep starting the day with "I heard something on NPR that I think you'd find interesting." You challenge me to look at the world and the people in it from every angle, and to put the pieces of the puzzle together. Thank you for being the man you are today. I'm a lucky lady.

Sal would like to thank Bonnie Ulman for always reminding me that I am smarter than I think I am and for involving me in and apprenticing me through *Hustle*. I thank my much-missed mom for constantly referring to the Great Depression throughout my upbringing. I had no idea how much I'd need those tips over the past four years and especially during the last four months. I thank my many clients and colleagues over the years who helped me hone my expertise in the marketing-to-moms and women's arena. You know who you are. A proper English toast to my economist friend Wayne Gantt for answering all my questions about charts that included the words "Non Farm Employment" and for tutoring me on economics. To my researcher friend Greg Rathjen of Marketecture, I appreciate the long and rambling discussions about brand relationships. Thank you to Patricia Wilson of Brand Cottage for her always brilliant insights about how to engage women consumers. To my girlfriends and to my daughter Bradley's girlfriends, thank you for having such a genuine interest in the book. For my son Henley, thanks for keeping it real by reminding me, "Some moms bake cookies. Some moms edit papers. You edit papers good." A "Good Dog" to Watson for constantly warming my feet as I typed, and real gratitude to my husband Brad for keeping the technology humming and for his long-time commitment to my success.

Endnotes

Chapter 1

1. Christopher J. Goodman and Steven M. Mance, "Employment Loss and the 2007-09 Recession: An Overview," *Monthly Labor Review*, 134 (4): 3, 2011.

2. Jesse Bricker, Arthur B. Kennickell, Kevin B. Moore and John Sabelhouse with assistance from Samuel Ackerman, Robert Argento, Gerhard Fries and Richard A. Windle, "Changes in U.S. Family Finances from 2007 to 2010: Evidence from the Survey of Consumer Finances" *Federal Reserve Bulletin,* June 2012, Vol 98, No. 2, p.1.

3. Goodman and Mance, p. 9

4. Cynthia R. Cohen, "Keep an Eye Out For . . . the Top Ten Consumer Trends of 2006," Chiefmarketer.com, January 6, 2006, (http://chiefmarketer.com/consumer_trends_01062006).

5. "Focus on Consumer Trends 2005: What They Want and Why," *Travel Weekly*, August 26, 2005, (http://www.travelweekly.com/Travel-News/Travel-Agent-Issues/Focus-on-Consumer-Trends-2005--What-they-want,-and-why/?page=2)

6. Michael J. Silverstein, Neil Fiske, *Trading Up: Why Consumers Want New Luxury Goods—and How Companies Create Them,* Penguin Group, 2005. p.3.

7. Goodman and Mance, p.4.

8. Benjamin Schwarz, "Life In (And After) Our Great Recession," *The Atlantic*, October 2009, (http://www.theatlantic.com/magazine/archive/2009/10/life-in-and-after-our-great-recession/307651/).

9. Jonathan V. Last, "America's Baby Bust," *The Wall Street Journal*, February 12, 2013, (http://online.wsj.com/article/SB10001424127887323375204578270053387770718.html).

10. Kathy Warbelow and Frank Bass, "Young U.S. Adults Flock to Parents' Homes Amid Economy," *Bloomberg*, September 26, 2012, (http://www.bloomberg.com/news/2012-09-25/young-adults-flock-to-parents-homes-amid-sour-economy.html).

11. Warbelow and Bass

Chapter 2

1. John Gottman, "John Gottman on Trust and Betrayal," October 28, 2011, (http://greatergood.berkeley.edu/article/item/john_gottman_on_trust_and_betrayal).
2. American Marketing Association, Dictionary, (http://www.marketingpower.com/_layouts/dictionary.aspx?dletter=b).
3. Gary L. Singer and Jeffrey T. Resnick, "Leveraging the Non-Conscious to Drive Transformational Growth, Buyology.com, (http://www.buyologyinc.com/MindLink_White_Paper.pdf).
4. Loretta Graziano Breuning, Ph.D., Psychology Today, July 18, 2011, (http://www.psychologytoday.com/blog/greaseless/201107/your-buttons-turn-real-neurochemicals).
5. Singer and Resnick
6. Ekaterina Walter, "The Top 30 Stats You Need to Know When Marketing to Women," *TNW*, January 23, 2013, (http://thenextweb.com/socialmedia/2012/01/24/the-top-30-stats-you-need-to-know-when-marketing-to-women/).

Chapter 3

1. Thad Reuter, "E-retail shoppers spent more than $186 billion last year, comScore says," *Internet Retailer*, February 7, 2013, (http://www.internetretailer.com/2013/02/07/e-retail-spending-jumps-15-2011).
2. She-conomy, "Marketing to Women: Quick Facts," (http://www.she-conomy.com/report/marketing-to-women-quick-facts).
3. Topics, "Groupon," Mashable, (http://mashable.com/category/groupon/)
4. Groupon, (http://www.groupon.com/about)
5. Rue La La, (http://www.ruelala.com)
6. Digby.com, "Mobile Commerce and Engagement Statistics," (http://www.digby.com/mobile-statistics/).
7. Ed Hadley, "11 Startling Stats About Customer Loyalty and Loyalty Programs," February 22, 2012, (http://blog.neolane.com/conversational-marketing/11-startling-stats-customer-loyalty-loyalty-programs/).
8. Belinda Luscombe, "Women Power: The Rise of the Sheconomy," *Time*, November 22, 2010, (http://www.time.com/time/magazine/article/0,9171,2030913,00.html).
9. Luscombe
10. Hadley

Chapter 4

1. Heidi Grant Halvorson, "Why Keeping Your Options Open is a Really, Really Bad Idea." May 29, 2011, (http://www.heidigranthalvorson.com/).

2. Halvorson

3. Gregory Berns, "In Hard Times, Fear Can Impair Decision-Making," *The New York Times*, December 6, 2008.

4. Barry Schwartz, as quoted in Betsy Wuebker, "Keeping Your Options Open Will Cost You," March 19, 2012, passingthru.com, (http://passingthru.com/2012/03/keeping-your-options-open-will-cost-you/).

Chapter 5

1. Francine Jay, "The Minsumer Movement: A Quiet Revolution," April 6, 2010, missminimalist.com, (http://www.missminimalist.com/2010/04/the-minsumer-movement-a-quiet-revolution/).

2. Academy of Nutrition and Dietetics, "Nationwide Survey on Family Eating Behaviors and Physical Activity Reveals Positive Changes and Opportunities," press release, November 9, 2010, (http://www.eatright.org/media/content.aspx?id=6442459599#.UU3JGhc3sxE).

3. "What That Car Really Costs to Own," ConsumerReports.org, August 2012, (http://www.consumerreports.org/cro/2012/12/what-that-car-really-costs-to-own/index.htm).

4. Mini, (http://www.miniusa.com/#/MINIUSA.COM-m)

5. Brad Tuttle, "Jalopy Nation? The Average Car on the Road Has Never Been Older," January 18, 2012, (http://business.time.com/2012/01/18/jalopy-nation-the-average-car-on-the-road-has-never-been-older/).

6. "Hard times bring on 'Lipstick Effect', PhysOrg.com, January 28, 2009, (http://phys.org/news152385593.html).

7. The Good Cook, (http://www.thegoodcook.com/bestselling-books.html)

8. Judy Muller, "Women Design Female-Friendly Power Tools," ABCNEWS.com, November 22, 2012, (http://abcnews.go.com/WNT/story?id=129999&page=1#.UVCIzkbCRdA)

9. Elizabeth Holmes, "More Women Try This at Home," WSJ.com, May 17, 2012, (http://online.wsj.com/article/SB10001424052702303448404577408124044457072.html)

Chapter 6

1. Sarah Kliff and Lena H. Sun, "Planned Parenthood says Komen decision causes donation spike," *The Washington Post*, February 1, 2012,

(http://articles.washingtonpost.com/2012-02-01/national/35445542_1_lee-fikes-karen-handel-breast-health-emergency-fund).

2. Jeffrey Kottler, Ph.D., as quoted in Anne Becker, PsychologyToday.com, July 1, 2003, (http://www.psychologytoday.com/articles/200307/what-makes-activist)

3. Andrea Chang, "Angie's List Has Strong First Day . . .," *The Los Angeles Times*, November 18, 2011, (http://articles.latimes.com/2011/nov/18/business/la-fi-angies-list-20111118).

4. Associated Press, "Women design concept car for Volvo," *USA Today*, March 2, 2004, (http://usatoday30.usatoday.com/money/autos/2004-03-02-ycc_x.htm).

5. Maddy Dychtwald, "Transformers and The Automotive Industry," Forbes.com, May 18, 2010, (http://www.forbes.com/2010/05/18/women-auto-industry-influence-forbes-woman-leadership-car-dealers.html).

6. Steve Olenski, "Nearly One Third of Online Consumers Trust a Stranger Over a Brand," Forbes.com, January 3, 2013, (http://www.forbes.com/sites/marketshare/2013/01/03/nearly-one-third-of-online-consumers-trust-a-stranger-over-a-brand/)

7. Marisa Grimes, "Nielsen: Global Consumer Trust in Earned Advertising Grows In Importance," Nielsen.com, May 10, 2012, (http://www.nielsen.com/us/en/press-room/2012/nielsen-global-consumers-trust-in-earned-advertising-grows.html)

8. National Newspaper Association, "Survey: Community papers still tops for local news," February 25, 2013, (http://nnaweb.org/article?articleTitle=survey-community-papers-still-tops-for-local-news--1361822263--502--1top-story).

9. National Newspaper Association

Chapter 7

1. "Have a Wet Cell Phone? Here's What to Do," HuffingtonPost.com, November 27, 2012, (http://www.huffingtonpost.com/2012/11/27/cell-phone-toilet_n_2198240.html).

2. "Zappos Takes a Close Look at Consumers' Mcommerce Patterns," February 22, 2013, (http://www.emarketer.com/Article/Zappos-Takes-Close-Look-Consumers-Mcommerce-Patterns/1009685).

3. "The Best and Worst of Mobile Connectivity," Pew Internet and American Life Project," Part IV, Cell Phone Attachment and Etiquette, November 20, 2012, (http://pewinternet.org/Reports/2012/Best-Worst-Mobile/Part-IV/Your-cell-phone-and-you.aspx).

4. Luisa Dillner, "Love by numbers," *The Guardian*, June 8, 2007, (http://www.guardian.co.uk/lifeandstyle/2007/jun/09/familyandrelationships).

5. "Mobile Spurs Digital Coupon User Growth," emarketer.com, January 31,

2013, (http://www.emarketer.com/Article/Mobile-Spurs-Digital-Coupon-User-Growth/1009639).

6. "You Tube 2012 Ads Leaderboards," Google, (http://www.thinkwithgoogle.com/insights/featured/youtube-leaderboard-2012/).

7. Todd Wasserman, "Chipotle's First National TV Ad Will Be a 2-Minute YouTube Video," mashable.com, February 10, 2012, (http://mashable.com/2012/02/10/chipotle-first-tv-ad-youtube/).

8. Forbes.com (http://www.forbes.com/power-women/list/)

9. Amanda Fortini, "O Pioneer Woman!," *The New Yorker*, pg. 5. May 9, 2011, (http://www.newyorker.com/reporting/2011/05/09/110509fa_fact_fortini?currentPage=5)

10. Kiri Blakeley, "Dooce's Dilemma," Forbes.com, July 15, 2009, (http://www.forbes.com/2009/07/15/dooce-heather-armstrong-forbes-woman-power-women-blog.html).

11. Amanda Fortini.

Chapter 8

1. Caitlin McDevitt, "Depression and The Recession: Cymbalta Sales Are on the Rise" *The Washington Post*, August 30, 2009, (http://articles.washingtonpost.com/2009-08-30/business/36831637_1_depressed-workers-effexor-antidepressants).

2. Benjamin Brafman, "Alcohol Addiction Rehab Facilities Must Prep for an Increase in Admissions in the Economic Downturn," ezinearticles, February 24, 2013, (http://ezinearticles.com/?Alcohol-Addiction-Rehab-Facilities-Must-Prep-for-an-Increase-in-Admissions-in-the-Economic-Downturn&id=6684115)

3. Vicki Morwitz, as quoted in Stephanie Clifford and Andrew Martin, "In Time of Scrimping, Fun Stuff Is Still Selling," *The New York Times*, September 23, 2011, (http://www.nytimes.com/2011/09/24/business/consumers-cut-back-on-staples-but-splurge-on-indulgences.html?_r=0).

4. "Yogurt's Growth Primarily Sources to Young Adults and In-Home Breakfast, Reports NPD," npd.com, January 29, 2013, (https://www.npd.com/wps/portal/npd/us/news/press-releases/yogurts-growth-primarily-sources-to-young-adults-and-in-home-breakfast-reports-npd/)

Chapter 9

1. Terry Weiss, "Major Crash Ahead for US Investors," Moneymorning.com, February 25, 2013, (http://moneymorning.com/ob-article/jim-rogers-major-crash-ahead.php#.UTjx0KXipLQ).

2. "J.C. Penney Company, Inc. Reports 2012 Fiscal Fourth Quarter and Full Year Results," JC Penney Website, Investor Relations, February 27, 2013,

(http://ir.jcpenney.com/phoenix.zhtml?c=70528&p=irol-newsCompanyArticle).

3. Zoe Chace, "Sales Are Like Drugs. What Happens When A Store Wants a Customer to Quit?" npr.org, Planet Money, March 1, 2013, (http://www.npr.org/blogs/money/2013/03/01/173203739/sales-are-like-drugs-what-happens-when-a-store-wants-customers-to-quit).

4. Joanna Glasner, "Why Webvan Drove Off a Cliff," *Wired*, July 10, 2001, (http://www.wired.com/techbiz/media/news/2001/07/45098).

5. She-conomy

6. "More Employers Blocking Access to Shopping Sites," njbiz.com, November 22, 2011, (http://www.njbiz.com/article/20111122/NJBIZ01/111129957/-1/dailyArchive/Survey:-More-employers-blocking-access-to-shopping-sites).

7. Amy Gage, "'The Great American Pastime' is shopping, says history professor in new book," *St. Olaf College News*, December 5, 2003, (http://www.stolaf.edu/news/index.cfm?fuseaction=newsdetails&id=1871).

8. Rachel King, , "Survey: 52% of consumers are overwhelmed by daily deal emails," *Between the Lines*, zdnet.com, June 20, 2011, (http://www.zdnet.com/blog/btl/survey-52-of-consumers-are-overwhelmed-by-daily-deal-emails/51023).

Chapter 10

1. "It's not Easy Being Green," written by Joseph Raposo, CTN

2. "African-American Consumers: Still Vital, Still Growing 2012," p. 4, nielsen.com, September, 29, 2012, (http://www.nielsen.com/us/en/reports/2012/african-american-consumers--still-vital--still-growing-2012-repo.html).

3. Selig Center for Economic Growth, "The Multicultural Economy 2012," terry.uga.edu, (http://www.terry.uga.edu/selig/publications/multicultural_economy.html).

4. Mary Lorenz, "10 Predictions in 10 Years: How the 2020 Workplace will Affect You," thehiringsite.com, July 1, 2010, (http://thehiringsite.careerbuilder.com/2010/07/01/10-predictions-in-10-years-how-the-2020-workplace-will-affect-you/).

Index

"editing life," 40
"latency response," 18
"minsumer," 41
"Sheconomy," 28
"slasher" workforce, 76–77
"the deal", 21–29, 83–84
    daily deals, 22, 64, 83
2020, 89–91

A

Abramson, Jill, 66
advertising, 47, 58–60, 64–65, 76, 86
affluence, 4
African American women, 2, 90–91
AirBnB.com, 48
Aldi, 29, 37
Amazon, 19, 37
American Dietetic Association
  Foundation, 44
American Dream, 3
Angie's List, 56
Apple, Inc., 37, 80
Armstrong, Heather B., 67
Asian women, 2, 12–13, 35, 58, 91
attitudes toward recession, 12–13, 14
    by age, 24 and 29, 2,
    by age 39–45, 11
    by age 51–60, 11, 13, 36–37, 58
    by age 46–50, 35
    by race and ethnicity, 2, 12, 15, 35,
    36–37, 58

automobile ownership, 57
    cost of, 45
    age of cars, 45

B

Bank of America, 63
Bartlett, Marcy, 72
Berns, Gregory, 34
Bird, Jackie, 37–38, 59
Boomer women, 85–86
Bradsdeals.com, 43, 64, 65
Brand Cottage, 64
brand loyalty, 17
    decline in, 14–15, 61–62
Breuning, Loretta Graziano, 17
Buyology, Inc., 18

C

Caucasian women, 2, 11, 90
ChiefMarketer.com, 3
Chipotle Mexican Grill, 65
Chobani, 74
Cleanhouse Challenge, 73–74
CNN, 60
Cohen, Cynthia R., 3
community newspapers, 60
Conrad, Cloud Q., 70
consignment stores, 42
consumer behavior, 23–26, 32–33
    choices, 38–39
    choice overload, 39

consumer power, 23–26, 43–44
consumer-brand relationship, 23, 26–27
cosmetic sales, 47–48
Costco, 25, 37, 47

D

DDB (ad agency), 59, 86
decision sets, 26
decision-making, x, 18, 31–36, 39
declining birthrate, 9
DeGeneres, Ellen, 66
Del Monte, 24
digital wallet, 85–86
discretionary spending, 25–26, 44–45, 72
Disney/ABC Television Group, 66
distrust, 12–14, 67
   In media, 59–60
*Doing Good: Passion and Commitment
   for Helping Others* (book), 54
do-it-yourself (DIY), 47–48
Dooce.com, 67
Dove, 18
Dreaming Cow, 74
Drummond, Ree, 67
Dyson vacuum cleaners, 75
Dyson, James, 75

E-F

economic downturn, 2, 6–7, 43
Edelman, Marion Wright, 53
Einstein, Albert, 41
eMarketer, 64
emotional default, xi
Epinions.com, 81
Facebook, 35, 60, 86
Farrell, James, 82
female influencers, 51–55
   examples of, 66
   markers of, 54
financial sacrifice, 12, 43, 70
Fiske, Neil, 4
Forbes magazine, 66

Forrester Research, 59
Freecycle, 82
friends, time with, 70–73
frugality fatigue, 10, 70–72, 84–85
future, 89–91

G

Gaither, Lee, 62–63, 67–68
Garcia, Meredith, 46
Gardner, Sue, 66
Gibbs, Lois, 53
Gilbert, Dan, 34
Gilt.com, 25
Goodman, Christopher J., 2–3
Gottman Relationship Institute, 14
Gottman, John, 13–14
Great Depression (1920s–1930s), ix, 7
Great Recession, x 1–4, 12, 27, 41, 67
   severity and duration, 2–3
   similarities to Great Depression,
      7–9, 46
   years leading to, 3–6
Great Repression, 10
Greater Good Science Center, 14
Green lifestyle, ix, 48–49, 69–70, 73–74,
   81
Groupon, 22–23, 83

H

Hallmark, 18
Halvorson, Heidi Grant, 33–34
HBO Entertainment, 66
Hempel, Peter, 86
Hicks, Angie, 56
Hispanic women (Latinas), 2, 15, 36,
   37–38, 58
home décor, 46–47
home improvement, 47–48
Honda, 37
household economy, xi, 2, 28, 43–44
housing growth, 3
Howard, Clark, 43
Huffington, Arianna, 66

Hustle economy, 28–29

I-J-K

Iconoclast (book), 34–35

Iida, Aki, 61

inside information, 25

Instagram, 65

integrated marketing, 26, 30, 36–38

inter-generational workplace, 90

It Sucked and Then I Cried (book), 67

Jaguar, 45

Jay, Francine, 40

JC Penney, 80

Johnson, Ron, 80

Joya no Kane, 40

Kellogg's, 37

Kottler, Jeffrey, 54

L

LiveWire Research, 2

LivingSocial, 22

local media influence, 60

Love Canal, 53

loyalty programs, 26–27

Luxury Marketing Council, 24

Lynd, Helen Merrell, 8

Lynd, Robert S., 8

M

Maid Brigade, 69

Mance, Steven, 2–3

market catastrophe, 2–3

market correction, 2–3

marketing strategies, 20, 29–30, 37–39,
   49–50, 55, 57–58, 75–76, 78–88
      advertising, 64–65
      consistency, 18, 20, 29–30, 55
      lessons for post-recession world, 79
      permission to trade down, 49–50
      tools for decision-making, 35–36
      solution-oriented content, 36

Maseng, Nancy, 70–71

mass collaboration, 55–56

Massage Envy, 72

Mayer, Marissa, 51

McDonald's, 37

meals eaten at home, 44

media use by consumers, 64–66

Middletown in Transition (book), 8

MINI Cooper, 45

MissMinimalist.com, 41

Mohammed, Rafi, 80

Monthly Labor Review, 2

Morning Edition/Planet Money, 80

Morwitz, Vicki G., 72

multi-cultural workplace, 90–91

multi-generational households, 9

multiple shopping channels, 26, 30

Murphy, Melissa, 24, 30

N-O

Naegle, Sue, 66

National Newspaper Association, 60

New American Dimensions, 90

new household formation, 9

Newberry, Allen, 48

Nielsen 2012 Global Trust in Advertising
   report, 59

Nike, 65

NPD Group, 74

Nucifora, Alf, 23

Olsson, Hans-Olov, 57

One Kings Lane, 25

*One Nation Under Goods: Malls and
   the Seductions of American Shopping*
   (book), 82

overspending, 26

P-Q-R

Panera Bread, 27

Pascal, Amy, 66

Patch.com, 60

Pepsi, 65

Pew Internet & American Life Project,
   62, 67

Pinterest, 60

Planned Parenthood, 52
Procter & Gamble, 37
Progressive Insurance (Flo), 86
Psychology Today, 17, 54
Publix market, 18, 63
Real Simple magazine, 73–74
Red Bean Society, 37, 59, 90
Robert Half Technology, 81–82
Rue La La, 25

S
Sam's Club, 25
Schwartz, Barry, 38
Schwarz, Benjamin, 8
screens (laptop, phone, TV), 61–68
Sephora, 27
Seventh Generation, 73
Share, 82
sharing (cars, equipment, etc.), 48–49
Silverstein, Michael J., 4
Simmermon, Robert, 31–32, 38, 42
simplicity, 42–49
Sodastream, 74
solutions, 27–28
Sony Pictures Television, 66
Southwest Airlines, 18
Staples, 27
Starbucks, 33
StarKist, 24
State Farm Insurance, 59
Stumbling on Happiness (book), 34
surprises, 87–88
Susan G. Komen for the Cure, 52
sustainability, 49
Sweeney, Anne, 66

T
Target, 37
technology, 53, 60–68, 85
The Atlantic, 8
The Dump, 47

The Guardian, 62
The Haystack Group, 31, 38, 54
The Milton Sweet Tea Socieety, 56
The New York Times, 66, 72
The Paradox of Choice: Why More is Less
(book), 38
The Pioneer Woman, 67
The Point, 22
The Psychology of Goals (book), 34
TheFashionList.com, 46
TheGoodCook.com, 46
Tide, 37
Time magazine, 4, 28, 60
Trader Joe's, 47
Trading Up: The New American Luxury
(book), 4–5
transaction vs. relationship, 15–18, 40
    attributes of excellent transactions,
    19
transit, 48–49
Travel Weekly magazine, 4
Twitter, 35, 67, 86

U-V-W-X-Y-Z
USA Today, 57
Volkswagen, 65
Volvo, 57
Von Maur department stores, 29
Walmart, 37
wardrobe changes, 46–47
Webvan, 81–82
WikiHow, 33
Wikimedia Foundation, 66
Wilson, Brad, 43–44
Wilson, Patricia, 64
Yesawich, Pepperdine, Brown &
    Robinson/Yankelovich Leisure Travel
    Monitor (survey), 4
yogurt, 74
YouTube, 35, 65, 86
Zappos, 34, 61
Zulily.com, 25–26

About the Authors

Bonnie Ulman

Bonnie Ulman is president of The Haystack Group, a strategic communications and consumer insights firm based in Atlanta. Co-author of a leading book about marketing to mothers, *Trillion-Dollar Moms: Marketing to a New Generation of Mothers*, Bonnie is considered a pioneer and nationally recognized expert in the fields of marketing-to-moms and marketing-to-women. She is a frequent speaker and media commentator and Bonnie's research and insights have been featured in various media outlets, including *The New York Times, Go Magazine, Bloomberg News, Atlanta Journal-Constitution, FamilyFun*, and others. Her perspective on the day-to-day issues impacting women has helped shape the content and programming created for television, online and print media. Backed by more than 25 years experience in brand-building and consumer insights, she has helped companies such as Wyeth Consumer Healthcare, American Express, Maid Brigade, Best Buy and Coca-Cola connect with their audiences to impact their bottom line.

Sal Kibler

Prior to starting her firm, Whole Brain Solutions, Sal held executive leadership positions in several of Atlanta's top advertising and marketing firms, including The Haystack Group, Inc. With a special interest in deciphering the code for what makes women and girls tick, Sal parlayed her marketing and advertising expertise into successful campaigns and brand invigorations for a range of clients, including Vanity Fair intimates, Nature's Own Bread, Russell Athletic Women's Division, Cox Communications, The Atlanta Women's Foundation, and The Georgia Coalition for Nutrition Education. She has been featured in *The New York Times*, *The Atlanta Business Chronicle*, *Atlanta Woman*, and *Go Magazine*. She has been named one of the "Women to Watch," and as head of one of Atlanta's "Fastest-Growing Women-owned Firms" by *The Atlanta Business Chronicle*, and to the *ADWEEK* Dream Team.